Day Walks in the LakeDistrict

20 circular routes on the Lakeland Fells

VERTEBRATE PUBLISHING

Design and production by Vertebrate Publishing, Sheffield
www.v-publishing.co.uk

Day Walks in the LakeDistrict

20 circular routes on the Lakeland Fells

Written by
Stephen Goodwin

Day Walks in the LakeDistrict

20 circular routes on
the Lakeland Fells

VG Copyright © 2009 **Vertebrate Graphics Ltd** and **Stephen Goodwin**

VP First published in 2009 by **Vertebrate Publishing**.
Reprinted in 2013 with minor amendments.

ISBN 978-1-906148-12-6

Cover photo by **Stephen Goodwin**: Great Langdale seen from above Chapel Stile.
Back cover photo by **David Chadwick**: Wast Water and Great Gable.

All other photography by **Stephen Goodwin** unless otherwise credited.

All maps reproduced by permission of Ordnance Survey on behalf
of The Controller of Her Majesty's Stationery Office.
© Crown Copyright. 100025218

Design by Nathan Ryder, production by Jane Beagley.
www.**v-graphics**.co.uk

VERTEBRATE PUBLISHING

MIX
Paper from
responsible sources
FSC
www.fsc.org   FSC® C016973

Printed in China.

Contents

*Shortcut available

TARN BY LANG HOW, NEAR GRASMERE (WALK 12)

Introduction

The Lake District is the only corner of England that can truly be said to be mountainous. Within the 885 square miles of the Lake District National Park is the country's highest peak, Scafell Pike, and its longest and deepest lakes, Windermere and Wast Water respectively. Yet it isn't these superlatives that make Lakeland special so much as its harmonious blend of rugged upland – beetling crags reflected in teardrop tarns – with a valley landscape of lakes, pasture, stone barns and white-painted farmhouses. The 20 walks in this guide explore the very best of it.

Whether or not there is any true wilderness left in England in the 21st century is a debate for philosophers. There is certainly a sense of wildness in the deep cwms abutting the Scafells, the Helvellyn range and High Street, and one of remoteness on the open fell tops. Although the national park gets some 12 million visitors per year, as I re-walked the routes included here I didn't encounter more than a score of people on any trail, save for the circuit of Derwent Water.

Even on Scafell Pike, on a day of uninterrupted sunshine, there were only a handful of fellow pilgrims; mind you, the temperature was well below freezing and the summit cairn an ice sculpture. Crystal air rendered Great Gable in high definition, while the Isle of Man rose in outline from the Irish Sea. Such are the rewards of walking in the Lake District. Red deer flowing over the quieter eastern fells, red squirrels in the northern woods, ravens, and perhaps an osprey seen from the ascent of Ullock Pike; this is their territory.

The guide is divided up into four geographical sections and in each are walks of different character, including, for the adventurous, the Lake District's best known scrambles – *Striding Edge* on Helvellyn and *Sharp Edge* on Blencathra. Should you complete every walk in the book you will have ascended 16,628 metres – almost the height of Everest and Nuptse put together. Better still, you will have had some truly memorable days out.

Stephen Goodwin

Acknowledgements

The author would like to thank the following people for their help:

Julian Cooper for good company in sun and sleet, Steve Lenartowicz and Dave Hellier for casting an experienced eye over the walk directions, and particularly my wife Lucie for her company, encouragement and support, on and off the hills.

About the walks

All the walks are 'day' walks in the sense that they take 4 to 8 hours at an unhurried pace. In character they include lakeside and valley tracks, well-worn paths on fell sides and broad ridges (the majority could be so described) to indistinct lines across moorland and on stony mountain tops.

Two of the walks include the option of ridge scrambles – *Striding Edge* on Helvellyn and *Sharp Edge* on Blencathra. Both are exposed and the scene of frequent accidents. They should only be attempted by competent scramblers with a head for heights and who understand the risk.

The **summary** and **route description** for each walk should be studied carefully before setting out on a walk.

All the walks are within the capabilities of a reasonably fit walker, but bear in mind that nearly all include several hundred metres of ascent – almost 1,500m in one case, higher than Ben Nevis.

Walk times

The time given for each walk is on the generous side and based on the *'walked experience'*. There is some allowance for snack breaks and photo stops, but prolonged lunches should be added in.

Navigation

For most walks in this guide, following the route description in combination with the route map provided should be sufficient. However it is recommended you carry with you the appropriate *Ordnance Survey Explorer* series map as a back up. These are shown for each walk. The Lake District is covered by four maps in the 1:25,000 series:

Ordnance Survey Explorer OL4 (1:25,000) The English Lakes, North-western area
Ordnance Survey Explorer OL5 (1:25,000) The English Lakes, North-eastern area
Ordnance Survey Explorer OL6 (1:25,000) The English Lakes, South-western area
Ordnance Survey Explorer OL7 (1:25,000) The English Lakes, South-eastern area

For fell top and moorland walks a reasonable level of map reading ability and competence in the use of a compass is strongly advised. If you possess a GPS (Global Postioning System) this can be a useful navigational aid in locating your position. However it is not a remedy for poor navigational skills.

Mobile phones

There is no mobile phone reception over much of the area covered by the 20 walks. You are thereby liberated from the phone's tyranny, but are also without its reassurance.

Footpaths and rights of way

All the walks in this guide follow public rights of way or other routes with public access, including *'permitted'* or *'concession'* footpaths.

Safety

It is strongly advised that appropriate footwear is used – walking boots designed to provide stability and security on uneven and slippery terrain. A waterproof, windproof jacket is essential and waterproof overtrousers or trousers are strongly recommended. Sufficient insulating clothing should also be worn or carried, that is appropriate to the type of walk planned and the time of year.

Trekking poles are a definite asset since they provide greater stability and security on steep ground or slippery footpaths, thereby lessening the chances of an accident resulting from difficult terrain.

On the high fell walks emergency rations should be carried in the event of the weather causing problems or an unplanned night out!

Mountain Rescue

In case of accident or similar need requiring mountain rescue assistance, **dial 999** and ask for **POLICE – MOUNTAIN RESCUE**. Be prepared to give a 6-figure grid reference of your position in the case of a moorland location.

The Countryside Code

Be safe – plan ahead

Even when going out locally, it's best to get the latest information about where and when you can go; for example, your rights to go onto some areas of open land may be restricted while work is carried out, for safety reasons or during breeding seasons. Follow advice and local signs, and be prepared for the unexpected.

» Refer to up-to-date maps or guidebooks.
» You're responsible for your own safety and for others in your care, so be prepared for changes in weather and other events.
» There are many organisations offering specific advice on equipment and safety, or contact visitor information centres and libraries for a list of outdoor recreation groups.
» Check weather forecasts before you leave, and don't be afraid to turn back.
» Part of the appeal of the countryside is that you can get away from it all. You may not see anyone for hours and there are many places without clear mobile phone signals, so let someone else know where you're going and when you expect to return.

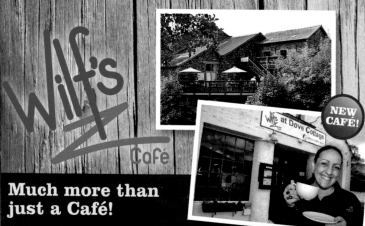

Wilf's Café

Much more than just a Café!

Buffets, Weddings, Outside catering, 'Wilf's Away' and Venue for hire for all occasions...

Wilf's Cafés offer great breakfasts, lunches, home-made cakes and afternoon teas plus daily meaty, veggie and fishy specials at Staveley; and cream teas at Dove Cottage. Our menus offer good wholesome, value for money meals that are all cooked on the premises. Local ingredients and specialities are used including Cumbrian meat and free range eggs sourced from a local farm.

We're also dog friendly – well behaved dogs are welcome in the Café and dog bowls are provided outside.

"Great little café. Wilf's is a superb café, the outside seating is well worth the visit to Staveley village. Really nice food at extremely reasonable prices."

"Wonderful food. I love the food here and the ambiance of the place."

Opening times	Opening times
Summertime weekdays 9am – 5pm	**Summertime weekdays** 9.30am – 5pm
weekends 8.30am – 5pm	**weekends** 9.30am – 5pm
Wintertime 9am – 5pm	**Wintertime** 9.30am – 5pm
7 days a week	7 days a week

Wilf's Café in Staveley
Mill Yard   Staveley   Kendal   LA8 9LR
T 01539 822329   F 01539 822969
E food@wilfs-cafe.co.uk

Wilf's Café in Grasmere
Dove Cottage   Grasmere   LA22 9SH
T 015394 35268
www.wilfs-cafe.co.uk

Leave gates and property as you find them
Please respect the working life of the countryside, as our actions can affect people's livelihoods, our heritage, and the safety and welfare of animals and ourselves.

» A farmer will normally leave a gate closed to keep livestock in, but may sometimes leave it open so they can reach food and water. Leave gates as you find them or follow instructions on signs; if walking in a group, make sure the last person knows how to leave the gates.
» In fields where crops are growing, follow the paths wherever possible.
» Use gates and stiles wherever possible – climbing over walls, hedges and fences can damage them and increase the risk of farm animals escaping.
» Our heritage belongs to all of us – be careful not to disturb ruins and historic sites.
» Leave machinery and livestock alone – don't interfere with animals even if you think they're in distress. Try to alert the farmer instead.

Protect plants and animals, and take your litter home
We have a responsibility to protect our countryside now and for future generations, so make sure you don't harm animals, birds, plants or trees.

» Litter and leftover food doesn't just spoil the beauty of the countryside, it can be dangerous to wildlife and farm animals and can spread disease – so take your litter home with you. Dropping litter and dumping rubbish are criminal offences.
» Discover the beauty of the natural environment and take special care not to damage, destroy or remove features such as rocks, plants and trees. They provide homes and food for wildlife, and add to everybody's enjoyment of the countryside.
» Wild animals and farm animals can behave unpredictably if you get too close, especially if they're with their young – so give them plenty of space.
» Fires can be as devastating to wildlife and habitats as they are to people and property – so be careful not to drop a match or smouldering cigarette at any time of the year. Sometimes, controlled fires are used to manage vegetation, particularly on heaths and moors between October and early April, so please check that a fire is not supervised before calling 999.

Keep dogs under close control

The countryside is a great place to exercise dogs, but it is owners' duty to make sure their dog is not a danger or nuisance to farm animals, wildlife or other people.

» By law, you must control your dog so that it does not disturb or scare farm animals or wildlife. You must keep your dog on a short lead on most areas of open country and common land between 1 March and 31 July, and at all times near farm animals.

» You do not have to put your dog on a lead on public paths as long as it is under close control. But as a general rule, keep your dog on a lead if you cannot rely on its obedience. By law, farmers are entitled to destroy a dog that injures or worries their animals.

» If a farm animal chases you and your dog, it is safer to let your dog off the lead – don't risk getting hurt by trying to protect it.

» Take particular care that your dog doesn't scare sheep and lambs or wander where it might disturb birds that nest on the ground and other wildlife – eggs and young will soon die without protection from their parents.

» Everyone knows how unpleasant dog mess is and it can cause infections – so always clean up after your dog and get rid of the mess responsibly. Also make sure your dog is wormed regularly.

Consider other people

Showing consideration and respect for other people makes the countryside a pleasant environment for everyone – at home, at work and at leisure.

» Busy traffic on small country roads can be unpleasant and dangerous to local people, visitors and wildlife – so slow down and, where possible, leave your vehicle at home, consider sharing lifts and use alternatives such as public transport or cycling. For public transport information, phone Traveline on 0871 200 2233.

» Respect the needs of local people – for example, don't block gateways, driveways or other entry points with your vehicle.

» By law, cyclists must give way to walkers and horse riders on bridleways.

» Keep out of the way when farm animals are being gathered or moved and follow directions from the farmer.

» Support the rural economy – for example, buy your supplies from local shops.

troll

ESTABLISHED 1965

A JOURNEY TO THE EDGE

www.trolluk.com

How to use this book

This book should provide you with all of the information that you need for an enjoyable, trouble free and successful walk. The following tips should also be of help:

1. We strongly recommend that you invest in the maps listed above on page ix. These are essential even if you are familiar with the area – you may need to cut short the walk or take an alternative route.

2. Choose your route. Consider the time you have available and the abilities/level of experience of all of members your party – then read the safety section of this guide.

3. We recommend that you study the route description carefully before setting off. Cross-reference this to your OS map so that you've got a good sense of general orientation in case you need an escape route. Make sure that you are familiar with the symbols used on the maps.

4. Get out there and get walking!

Maps, Descriptions, Distances

While every effort has been made to maintain accuracy within the maps and descriptions in this guide, we have had to process a vast amount of information and we are unable to guarantee that every single detail is correct.

Please exercise caution if a direction appears at odds with the route on the map. If in doubt, a comparison between the route, the description and a quick cross-reference to your OS map (along with a bit of common sense) should help ensure that you're on the right track. Note that distances have been measured off the map, and map distances rarely coincide 100% with distances on the ground. Please treat stated distances as a guideline only.

Ordnance Survey maps are the most commonly used, are easy to read and many people are happy using them. If you're not familiar with OS maps and are unsure of what the symbols mean, you can download a free OS 1:25,000 map legend from **www.v-outdoor.co.uk**

Here are a few of the symbols and abbreviations we use on the maps and in our directions:

 ROUTE STARTING POINT   SHORT CUT

 ROUTE MARKER   OPTIONAL ROUTE

PB = public bridleway; **PF** = public footpath; **GR** = grid reference.

Km/mile conversion chart

Metric to Imperial

1 kilometre [km]	1000 m	0.6214 mile
1 metre [m]	100 cm	1.0936 yd
1 centimetre [cm]	10 mm	0.3937 in
1 millimetre [mm]		0.03937 in

Imperial to Metric

1 mile	1760 yd	1.6093 km
1 yard [yd]	3 ft	0.9144 m
1 foot [ft]	12 in	0.3048 m
1 inch [in]		2.54 cm

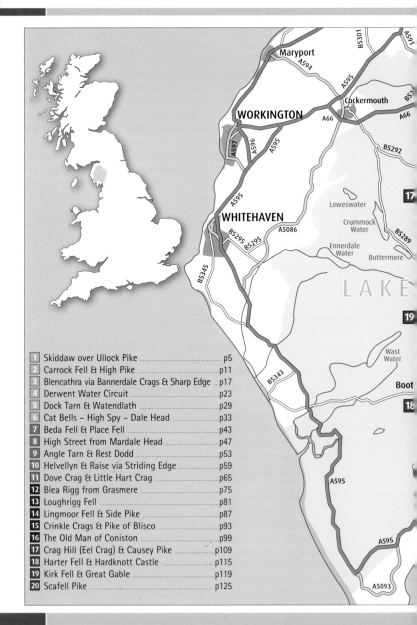

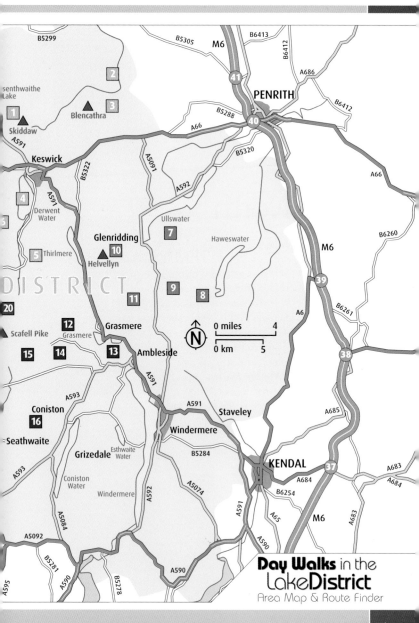

B5299

B5305

M6

B6413

B6412

2

senthwaithe Lake

1

Skiddaw

3

Blencathra

A591

Keswick

B5322

PENRITH

41

40

A686

B6412

B5288

A66

B5320

A66

A592

A5091

4

Derwent Water

5

A591

Ullswater

7

Haweswater

B6260

Glenridding

10

Helvellyn

5

Thirlmere

M6

39

DISTRICT

20

11

9

8

B6261

12

Grasmere

Scafell Pike

Grasmere

A6

15

14

13

Ambleside

N

0 miles 4

0 km 5

A591

A593

Coniston

16

A591

Staveley

A685

38

Seathwaite

Grizedale

Esthwaite Water

Windermere

B5284

KENDAL

A683

A593

Coniston Water

Windermere

A592

A5074

A684

37

A683

A5084

B6254

A591

M6

A683

A5092

A65

A590

B5581

B5278

A595

A590

A590

Day Walks in the Lake District
Area Map & Route Finder

SECTION 1

North

*This section covers two distinct areas –
the massif north of the A66 dominated by
Skiddaw and Blencathra, and the fells that
enclose Derwent Water and Borrowdale.
The Skiddaw group is predominantly
composed of a friable slate that has given
these grassy hills a smooth-sculpted profile.
Above Borrowdale are undulating fells clad
in bracken, heather and rough grasses.
There are the remains of old mines,
and red squirrels still inhabit the woods.
Keswick is the access town.*

CROSSING BANNERDALE BECK (WALK 3)

DERWENT WATER FROM SURPRISE VIEW (WALK 4)

SKIDDAW FROM THE WATCHES, BELOW ULLOCK PIKE

01 **Skiddaw over Ullock Pike** 10.8km/6.7miles

Woodland followed by broad mountain ridge approach to Lakeland's northern giant.

Mirehouse » Ling How » Ullock Pike » Longside Edge » Carlside Tarn » Skiddaw (931m) » Carl Side » White Stones » Dodd Wood » Mirehouse

Start

Pay and display car park by the Sawmill Tearoom at Mirehouse/Dodd Wood, 6km/4 miles north of Keswick on A591. GR: NY 235282.

The Walk

Skiddaw's easy gradient and proximity to Keswick made it an obvious goal for early tourists. Ascents for pleasure date back to the 17th century and in Victorian times the mountain was busy with guides, ponies and the portering of picnics. Once thought to be the highest mountain in England, despite demotion to fourth place it has lost none of its popularity.

The trick is to devise a route that avoids the tourist route slog from Keswick yet gains all the reward of the summit panorama – north across the Solway to Scotland and south across Lakeland. Hence our start from *Dodd Wood* – a vantage for watching the ospreys that nest above Bassenthwaite. After 2km we leave the wood's edge and ascend heather slopes to *Ling How*,

a hollow towards the northern end of the bow-profiled ridge of *Ullock Pike*. The 2km traverse is a treat, quite steep on shaley stepped rock as the Pike is neared, then easily over *Longside Edge* – at 734m the highest point on the ridge – before descending gently to *Carlside Tarn*.

From the little tarn, our line up *Skiddaw's* flank looks daunting. The 'path' is loose, steep and shaley, and requires care. But it's soon over and we can relax for a stroll north on the broad summit ridge to the trig' point (931m), the Solway and Southern Uplands laid out beyond. Imagine Wordsworth and Southey up here in August 1815 among a crowd of revellers, feasting on roast beef and rum as they celebrated the Battle of Waterloo around a bonfire of tar barrels.

Returning to *Carlside Tarn*, we turn southwest, over *Carl Side* itself and then down to *White Stones* where we turn west and steeply down to re-enter *Dodd Wood*. A forest track leads us back to the car park and a cuppa in the Old Sawmill.

SKIDDAW OVER ULLOCK PIKE

DISTANCE: 10.8KM/6.7MILES » **TOTAL ASCENT:** 920M/3,018FT » **START GR:** NY 235282 » **TIME:** ALLOW 5 HOURS **MAP:** OS EXPLORER OL4, THE ENGLISH LAKES NORTH-WESTERN AREA, 1:25000 » **REFRESHMENTS:** THE OLD SAWMILL TEAROOM AT THE MIREHOUSE CAR PARK START AND FINISH POINT, OPEN APRIL TO OCTOBER » **NAVIGATION:** ATTENTION NEEDED AT SUCCESSION OF JUNCTIONS NEAR START, THEN STRAIGHTFORWARD. CLEAR LINE ALONG CREST OF ULLOCK PIKE. IN POOR VISIBILITY CARE NEEDED IN PICKING THE DESCENT LINE FROM POINT 5 ON SKIDDAW.

SKIDDAW RISING BEYOND DERWENT WATER AND KESWICK

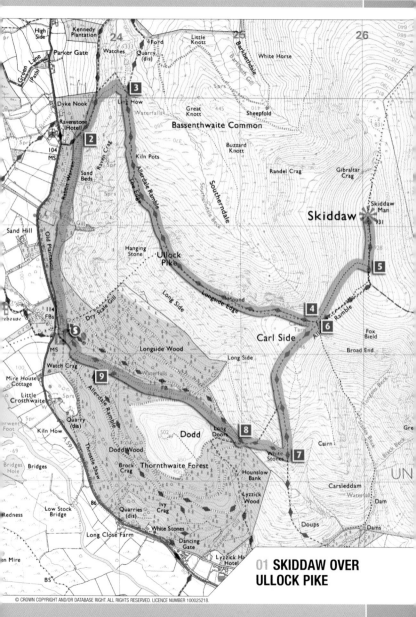

01 SKIDDAW OVER ULLOCK PIKE

Directions – Skiddaw over Ullock Pike

➏ From the car park, cross Skill Beck by a footbridge on the upstream side of the Sawmill Tearoom, as directed on a fingerpost pointing to *All Trails*. **Turn left** immediately over the footbridge, passing a trail marker post. Path curves down and then up to cross a forest road. **Bear left**, passing another marker post, on a rising path beneath pines. After 5mins on this, **bear left** on a path with low cliff on the uphill side and yellow marker post on the other. Path contours northward, ignore tracks dipping towards the main road.

2 A little over a mile (half an hour) from the car park, the path dips to join a track coming up from the left. **Turn right** on this and a minute later **bear right** up narrow path leading to a gate and onto the fell. Ascend steadily with fence on left to a brow at c250m. **Branch right** up fellside, heading NE and later SE towards skyline.

3 Path meets the ridge at Ling How (330m). **Turn southwards** and follow obvious path, climbing steadily up the ridge towards Ullock Pike (690m) – gained after about 1hr on the ridge. Continue along the crest to Longside Edge (734m), followed by a slight descent, keeping to the main path.

4 Carlside Tarn – this small pond marks an important junction. Route up (and down) Skiddaw is plain to see, ascending NE up shattered grey slate to the mountain's crest*. **Care** is needed on the skittery shale, especially on the descent; walking poles are a useful aid. We will be returning to Carlside Tarn after visiting Skiddaw.

> ☞ ***SC**: *Miss out ascent of Skiddaw and descend to car park as from instruction* **6**.

5 Ascent path meets the broad highway along the top of Skiddaw at a low crescent-shaped cairn/windbreak 200m south of the actual summit. Take note of this junction. Continue north to the summit (931m) then return to crescent junction and descend, **with care**, to Carlside Tarn.

6 From the tarn, take the path rising SW to the mound of Carl Side (746m) and then relentlessly down, trending southwards.

7 White Stones. **Turn right** (westwards) at the Stones on a contouring path for 1min to a cairn and **turn left**, descending steeply on a rough path, rightwards, aiming for a forestry road on a col (Long Doors) with the summit of Dodd beyond.

8 Cross style on to forestry road and **turn right** (NW). In 2mins road forks. **Take left branch**, post with green marker. From here the gravel road descends gently, Skill Beck on right in its valley. Keep to this angle, ignoring tracks branching up left.

9 After 1.5km (25 mins) the forest road curves left and a broad track **branches right** to continue the descent. Follow the latter, past a red and green marker post. In 5mins a path crossing is reached. **Turn right**, still following red and green markers, and another 5mins should see you back at the car park.

THE RIDGE OF ULLOCK PIKE – LONGSIDE EDGE

CARROCK FELL & HIGH PIKE

DISTANCE: 13.5KM/8.5MILES **» TOTAL ASCENT:** 620M/2,034FT **» START GR:** NY 354338 **» TIME:** ALLOW 5.5 HOURS
MAP: OS EXPLORER OL5, THE ENGLISH LAKES NORTH-EASTERN AREA, 1:25000 **» REFRESHMENTS:** QUAKER MEETING HOUSE
IN MOSEDALE, TEAS IN AFTERNOON, OTHERWISE NONE. NEAREST PUB, THE MILL INN, MUNGRISDALE **» NAVIGATION:** NO
DIFFICULTY AT VALLEY LEVEL, MUCH OF ROUTE ON QUIET LANE, HOWEVER STRETCHES ON THE RELATIVELY FEATURELESS PLATEAU
REQUIRE CARE IN MIST, PARTICULARLY WHERE SEVERAL TRACKS INTERSECT NEAR HIGH PIKE, AND MAP AND COMPASS WORK
MAY BE NECESSARY.

THE INFANT RIVER CALDEW IN MOSEDALE

By old mines and tumbling beck to open fell and Iron Age hill fort.

Stone Ends » Mosedale » Carrock Fell Mine » Grainsgill Beck » Lingy Hut » High Pike » Carrock Fell (662m) » Stone Ends

Start

Park on verge on west side of Mungrisdale-Hesket Newmarket road near overgrown pit below east flank of Carrock Fell. Gateway to Stone Ends Farm lies 100 yards south on opposite side of road. GR: NY 354338.

The Walk

Carrock Fell stands as a rugged bulwark at the north-east corner of the Lakeland fells. Topped by the remains of an Iron Age fort, its flanks were mined over centuries for copper, lead, barytes and precious tungsten.

We begin at Carrock's eastern foot, called, appropriately *Stone Ends*, follow the road south to *Mosedale* and branch west, passing an old Quaker meeting house, and into the unspoilt dale. Further along, the lane follows the River Caldew until we branch right on a mine track.

Only the foundations remain of the buildings of *Carrock Fell Mine*, last worked in 1981. But the bounty here will not have been forgotten, for Carrock is of strategic importance, a rare source of tungsten ore, used for hardening armour-piercing shells.

It is an incongruously violent thought to ponder as we pick our way up by lovely *Grainsgill Beck*, clear water hurrying between banks of heather and low mountain ash. The path becomes indistinct before joining a worn skyline track near the prominent bothy on *Lingy Hill*, a former shooting box tethered against the elements.

A fell top highway leads us north to the bare lookout of *High Pike* – Scotland beyond the Solway – from where we backtrack briefly before heading east across the occasionally boggy plateau to the rocky knoll that crowns *Carrock Fell*. The band of stones that ring the summit area are the remains of an Iron Age fort and it is said the Brigantes held out here against the Romans.

From Carrock's east top we descend through heather and bilberry, then steeply down the dry gully of *Further Gill*. Keep an eye open for the rapid silhouette of a peregrine falcon, which frequent the crags above *Stone Ends*.

CARROCK FELL SUMMIT

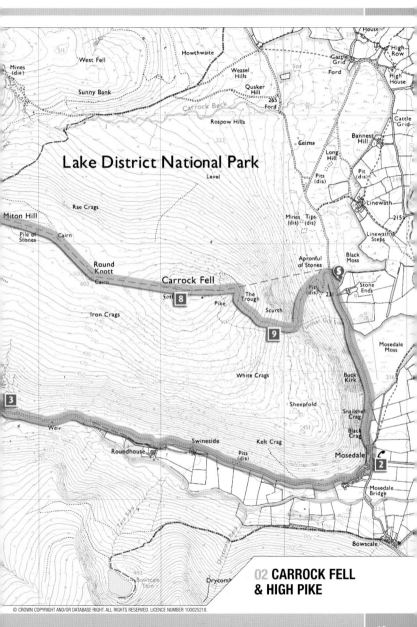

02 CARROCK FELL & HIGH PIKE

Directions – Carrock Fell & High Pike

⊙▸ From verge-side parking, walk south on roadside, passing gateway to Stone Ends Farm, for 1.5km to hamlet of **Mosedale**.

2 At Mosedale **turn right**, signposted *Swineside*, passing Quaker meeting house on left, and continue on lane for 3km, passing Swineside Farm and the Roundhouse.

3 **Turn right** up mine track, barrier to vehicles, signed *Bridleway to Miller Moss* and also marked with a yellow Cumbria Way roundel.

4 Remains of mine reached in 10mins. Cross Brandy Gill issuing from mine workings and follow track up hillside towards more workings. After 100m, where mine track bends back right, **branch left**, aiming up Grainsgill Beck. Path, boggy in places, follows right bank of beck (facing upstream) for 1.5km. Halfway along, jump a tributary stream, 'Arm o Grain', and keep to Grainsgill, ignoring faint path to right.

5 Path, boggy and braided, ascends towards where stream falls from notch in skyline. As this is reached, **bear right** on faint path. Box-like Lingy hut comes into view. **Bear right** again as more obvious path is reached and head to hut. (This bigger path would have been reached anyway had one continued through the notch.) After hut continue NNE on track (Cumbria Way).

6 Track breasts Hare Stones and descends slightly to saddle (1km from hut) crossed by several pathways. Ascend straight ahead (NNE) on worn turf line up High Pike.

7 **High Pike** (658m) – cairn, trig' point and slate bench. Descend directly south (following ascent line for 50m) cross fell track and curve around head of gullies above Drygill Beck to join good track. **Turn left** on this, undulating eastwards towards Carrock Fell. After Milton Hill track braids in boggy terrain but maintains its easterly course to stoney ramparts of Carrock.

8 **Carrock Fell** (662m) summit cairn and windbreak. Eastward on fell top, passing stones thought to be perimeter wall of fort, to cairn on edge of plateau. Descend steeply through rocks and bear right on path heading roughly SE through heather.

9 After tumbled shelter, path **turns left** through heather to the top of Further Gill gully. Eroded waist deep trench for about 10m. Step down into this or trample through the heather at its side. Descend steeply into gully, rough path zig-zagging. **Take extra care on skittery stones**. Trend leftwards across hillside to scree. Descend path in grass and bracken on left side of scree and on at easier angle to parking place.

OLD SLUICE IN GRAINSGILL BECK ABOVE CARROCK MINE

BLENCATHRA VIA BANNERDALE CRAGS & SHARP EDGE

DISTANCE: 14.5KM/9MILES » **TOTAL ASCENT:** 870M/2,854FT » **START GR:** NY 362303 » **TIME:** ALLOW 5.5 HOURS » **MAP:** OS EXPLORER OL5 THE ENGLISH LAKES, NORTH-EASTERN AREA, 1:25000 » **REFRESHMENTS:** THE MILL INN, MUNGRISDALE
NAVIGATION: IN MIST OR CLOUD, MAP AND COMPASS WORK MAY BE NEEDED TO GET THE CORRECT LINE OFF THE FLATTISH TOP OF BANNERDALE CRAGS. THIS COULD ALSO APPLY ON BLENCATHRA THOUGH THE PATHS ARE MUCH MORE OBVIOUS.

GETTING TO GRIPS WITH SHARP EDGE

03 **Blencathra via Bannerdale Crags & Sharp Edge**

14.5km/9miles

Riverside and ridges to one of Lakeland's most imposing summits. Optional airy scramble along Sharp Edge.

Mungrisdale » Bannerdale Crags » Scales Tarn » Sharp Edge » Blencathra (868m) » Scales Fell » River Glenderamackin » Mungrisdale

Start

Top end of Mungrisdale village by the phone box. (Parking here and also on road side at south end of the village.) GR: NY 362303.

The Walk

Blencathra's east flank, with the impressive arête of Sharp Edge projecting from a band of darks cliffs, is the unmistakable signal to motorists westbound on the A66 that they have arrived in England's mountains.

Approached from the roadside at Scales, Blencathra – or Saddleback to use its descriptive English name – is not the major undertaking it may at first appear as the road is already at 225 metres. By its simplest route, the top can be reached in a couple of hours. However, to make a decent day of it, we will start at the village of *Mungrisdale* and take a connoisseur's route by the *River Glenderamackin* and up the fine east ridge of *Bannerdale Crags*.

At the flat summit, *Blencathra* comes into view and we descend via the head of the deep valley of the upper Glenderamackin

to arrive eventually at *Scales Tarn*. Here a choice has to be made – whether to ascend via the rock scramble on *Sharp Edge* or by the easy path up the slope above the tarn's southern shore.

Sharp Edge is a notorious accident black spot. On the other hand, for the sure-footed and competent it is the most exhilarating way up Blencathra. All ways come together shortly before Blencathra's summit. The highest point is marked on the OS map as Hallsfell Top, overlooking the deep cut gullies and ridges that give the mountain its grand southern aspect, Derwent Water shimmers beyond.

The walk back to Mungrisdale is long – almost 5 miles – but we can relax; a well-made path curves down Scales Fell, a grassy trod takes us over the saddle above the Glenderamackin, and from there the river accompanies us back to the village, the prospect of the Mill Inn an added incentive.

SHARP EDGE

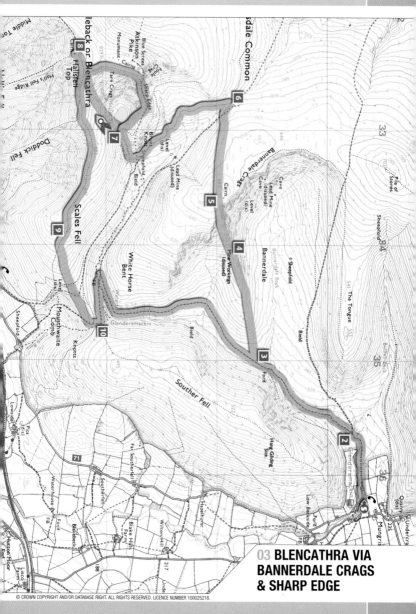

03 BLENCATHRA VIA BANNERDALE CRAGS & SHARP EDGE

Directions – Blencathra via Bannerdale Crags & Sharp Edge

➊ From phone box and signpost *PF Mungrisdale Common* follow track between cottages, through gate and on to common, continuing westwards, River Glenderamackin on left.

2 Just after fording side stream, Bullfell Beck, main track turns uphill. Instead **bear left** to continue on riverbank path for another 1km.

3 Immediately after fording Bannerdale Beck, **turn right** up bank and gain the broad foot of Bannerdale's east ridge. Grassy path ascends to old mine workings.

4 Shale path zigzags though workings and on up narrowing ridge, rocky in parts. Though too easy to qualify as a graded 'scramble', the ridge **requires care** and under snow or ice should only be attempted by those competent with ice axe and crampons.

5 At top of ridge, grassy path curves round above crags to cairn. Walk west to actual summit (683m) marked by a small pile of slate. (Blencathra now in view west.) Path curves rightwards and gently down to a junction on col (610m) between Bannerdale Crags and Blencathra.

6 At col, **turn left** on path angling down on west side of valley for 1km to Scales Beck. **Turn right**, upstream, and ascend on right bank of beck (facing up) to outflow from Scales Tarn.

7 **Sharp Edge** is the obvious serrated ridge above the north side of the tarn. Ascend the grassy spur that leads to the foot of the rocks. Keep on or close to the crest for the best scrambling. The trickiest bit is the descent to a notch where the ridge abuts the main mountain. Scrambling continues up headwall, most easily in the rough staircase of a broad groove, to the plateau. Path swings **leftwards** above the crags to join the Scales Fell track just before the summit.

 Warning: The rock along Sharp Edge is polished and requires great care when wet. Seemingly easier paths have been beaten on the north flank, but are misleading and potentially dangerous as the ridge must be gained at some point. Accidents are frequent.

Easy Alternative: For those not attracted to the scramble along Sharp Edge, cross the beck at the tarn outflow and take path up the fellside on **the south side of the tarn**. This joins the main Scales Fell track up Blencathra.

8 **Blencathra summit** (868m). Retrace steps and descend eastwards on Scales Fell path.

9 After 2km path forks. **Bear left** to continue down broad grassy nose to saddle between Mousthwaite Combe and Glenderamackin valley.

10 At lowest point of saddle, **turn left** and descend to River Glenderamackin. Cross footbridge and **turn right** on riverside path that leads eventually to outward route and on to Mungrisdale – 4km (2.5 miles) from footbridge to Mungrisdale.

CLOUD SEA; HALL'S FELL RIDGE, BLENCATHRA

LODORE FALLS, BORROWDALE

04 **Derwent Water Circuit** 16km/10miles

An easy circuit of one of England's most beautiful lakes.

Keswick Lakeside » Friar's Crag » Calfclose Bay » Lodore » Manesty Wood » Brandlehow Wood »
Fawe Park » Nichol End » Portinscale » Keswick » Lakeside

Start

Pay and display car park opposite Crow Park at Lakeside, Keswick.
GR: NY 265229.

The Walk

With only 150 metres of ascent over a distance of 10 miles, this lakeside circuit is pretty well level going. Easy underfoot and low lying, you could hold it in reserve for a day when cloud or rain envelopes the higher hills, but Derwent Water's unfolding delights deserve better than to be regarded as simply a wet weather option.

We start close by the *Keswick landing stages*, a busy spot for trippers and a reminder that this walk can be shortened by taking a launch to or from any of five other jetties around the lake (**www.keswick-launch. co.uk** for timetable). Putting aside temptation, we walk the short distance to the rocky promontory of *Friar's Crag*, a classic Lakeland viewpoint. John Ruskin regarded it as *"one of the three most beautiful scenes in Europe"*.

From the pine-clad headland we can survey our route – south along the bays, fringed by turns with pasture and woodland to *Lodore*, across meadow and marsh at the head of the lake – the boardwalk here is made from recycled plastic bottles – and then back through *Brandlehow Wood* and by *Fawe Park* to *Portinscale*.

Along the way, we could make a short diversion to see the famous Lodore Falls, much celebrated by the Romantics, though, as Keats found, an anti-climax in dry spells. And beneath the magnificent firs of Brandlehow, note the giant cupped hands, a sculpture in wood marking the centenary of the National Trust. Brandlehow was the NT's first acquisition in the Lake District.

All the while, the eye will be drawn back to the lake, its islands – including St Herbert's where the 7th century saint is said to have built a hermitage – and to the surrounding fells, Skiddaw and Blencathra to the north, the Jaws of Borrowdale and the Scafells to the south.

DERWENT WATER CIRCUIT

DISTANCE: 16KM/10MILES » **TOTAL ASCENT:** 150M/492FT » **START GR:** NY 265229 » **TIME:** ALLOW 4.5 HOURS
MAP: OS EXPLORER OL4, THE ENGLISH LAKES NORTH-WESTERN AREA, 1:25000 » **REFRESHMENTS:** NUMEROUS
THROUGH KESWICK AND IN THE LANDING STAGES AREA. ELSEWHERE ON ROUTE, MARY MOUNT HOTEL AND NICOL END
MARINA » **NAVIGATION:** ROUTE FOLLOWS PATHS ON OR CLOSE TO FORESHORE WITH DEVIATIONS 'INLAND' FROM HAWES
END TO PORTINSCALE AND THROUGH KESWICK.

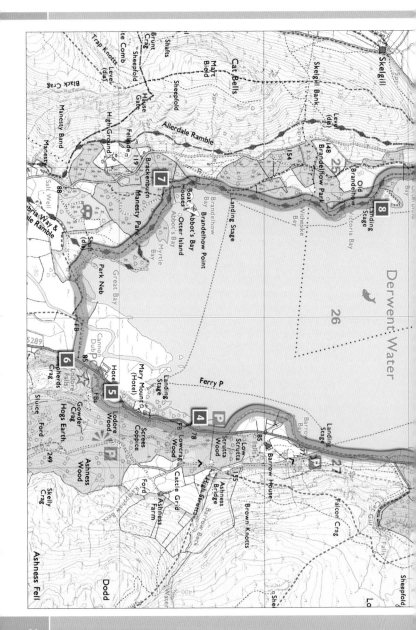

Skelgill

Trap Knotts
Level
(dis)

Black Crag

Brunt
Crag

Mart
Bield

Cat Bells

Skelgill Bank

Level
(dis)

Shafts

Sheepfold

Sheepfold

148
Brandelhow
Park

154

25

Old
Brandelhow

Victoria Bay

Landing
Stage

8

te Comb

Hause
Gate

High Ground

Fell area

Allerdale Ramble

Manesty Band

Manesty

Brackenburn

Manesty Park

Brandelhow
Bay

Brandelhow Point

Withesike
Bay

Derwent Water

Salt Well

89

mbria Way &
dale Ramble

7

Shaft
(dis)

Boat
Houses

Abbot's Bay

Otter Island

Abbot's Bay

Landing Stage

26

Park Neb

Myrtle
Bay

Great Bay

80

FB

5289

Cannon
Dub
P
85

Hotel
(Hotel)

Mary Mount
(Hotel)

Landing
Stage

6

odore
Falls
epherds
Crag

Sluice
Ford

Hogs Earth

249

5

FB

Lodore
Wood

Gowder
Crag

Ashness
Wood

Ferry P

P

4

Screes
Coppice

Lowcrag
Wood

Cattle Grid

Ashness
Ford

Ashness
Farm

Low
Scrutta
Wood

Scrutta
Wood

P

FB

78

High Scrutta Beck

Ashness
Bridge

Barrow
Bay

85

Barrow House

71

Brown Knots

Landing
Stage

27

Falcon Crag

Sheepfold

Skelly
Crag

Ashness Fell

Dodd

Ashness Fell

Lo

04 DERWENT WATER CIRCUIT

Directions – Derwent Water Circuit

➊ From the car park, walk past the front of the Theatre by the Lake and landing stages on a busy path south by lake to Friar's Crag viewpoint.

2 Friar's Crag. Retrace steps a few metres and **turn right** by Ruskin memorial amid pines and through gate at foot of the mound, curving around Strandshag Bay and into The Ings woodland.

3 At far side of wood, through gate and **turn right** on gravel track. Pass house on right, over cattle grid, follow path signed *Calfclose Bay*. For next 2.5km to Kettlewell car park follow shoreline path (just south of Calfclose Bay this is in a fringe of pine woods).

4 Kettlewell car park (not named on OS map, lies 500m north of Mary Mount Hotel). Cross the B5289 Borrowdale Road and follow path through woods, at first parallel with road. After Mary Mount Hotel (on opposite side of road) **bear left**, roundel on post signed *Lodore Fall*.

5 Path leads through trees to side of Lodore Hotel. At path T-junction **turn right** over footbridge to rear of hotel. (Left turn leads to Lodore Falls.) Through hotel yard to rejoin Borrowdale Road. Cross to pavement and **turn left**, passing public toilets on your right.

6 About 150m after toilets, **turn right** through gate – signposted *PF Manesty* and across water meadow to footbridge spanning the Derwent. Over this and onto board-walk crossing marsh. After boardwalk keep to good path curving north round end of lake; ignore paths branching left. Though gate into Manesty Park woodland.

7 At cottage, 'The Warren', **turn right** down lane, through gate signed *Abbot's Bay*. **Bear left** and through gate signed *Brandlehow & Keswick*. Pass cottage and after crossing stream on small footbridge **turn right** and through gate onto shoreline path, soon entering woods and passing Brandlehow jetty.

8 After 1km of beautiful woodland, through gate and **bear left** away from lake (shore path continues to viewpoint only). Soon through another gate. Stay on main path across field, past carved 'fish' bench, and up to iron gate. **Turn right** on lane sign-posted *Catbells & Keswick*. Pass Hawes End outdoor centre.

9 At junction in hollow, leave tarmac and **go through gate on right** on to path signed *Portinscale & Keswick*. Follow this northwards through trees, over field and more woods to pass Lingholm house on right.

10 Across driveway of Lingholm **bear right** down wallside and on to gateway of Fawepark house. **Take path to left** of 'The Lodge' gatehouse, signed *Nichol End & Portinscale*. Descend to Nicol End marina. (Good café on right.) **Turn left** to road, then **turn right** and follow road to Portinscale.

11 Portinscale. **Turn right** at bus stop, signed *PF to Keswick*, pass Derwent Water Hotel and on to footbridge over River Derwent.

12 About 150m after bridge, **turn right** through gate signed *PF to Keswick* and cross water meadows to road by River Greta. **Turn left** and then **right** at main road, to cross River Greta and enter Keswick. From the Moot Hall in the town centre, Lake Road (starting by the Old Keswickian chip shop) leads to the car park.

SUNSET OVER DERWENT WATER

SHEEPFOLD – AND KEY JUNCTION – BY STONETHWAITE BECK

05 Dock Tarn & Watendlath

9km/5.5miles

Oakwood, heather moor and secluded farmland on an easy round linking two tranquil tarns.

Rosthwaite » Stonethwaite Bridge » Willygrass Gill » Dock Tarn » Watendlath » Puddingstone Bank » Rosthwaite

Start

Small pay and display car park in lane to village hall and Yew Tree Farm tearoom, off B5289 Borrowdale road.
GR: NY 258149.

The Walk

Watendlath, with its sombre tarn, farm and emerald fields tucked in a side valley above Borrowdale, has been a tourist destination since the 18th century. Hugh Walpole immortalised it in the second of his *Herries* chronicles, *Judith Paris* (1931). Yet the hamlet remains unspoilt and Judith's fictional home, Fold Head Farm, very much an unprettified working farm. Most visitors approach by road – a lane up from B5289 beside Derwent Water – but we shall come over the moor via Dock Tarn.

From *Rosthwaite Bridge* we follow a bridleway southwards alongside Stonethwaite Beck, sharing this bit of the route with the Coast-to-Coast trail and the Cumbria Way. Beyond *Stonethwaite Bridge* we take off on our own, soon entering an oak wood beside *Willygrass Gill* and ascending steeply on an engineered staircase of rock steps.

Emerging from the wood at the well-named *Lingy End*, a promontory swathed in heather (ling), it is an opportunity to draw breath and take in the fine view south up Langstrath to Bowfell and its lofty neighbours. Our path now winds among the rocky knuckles and heathery bowls of the Knotts to *Dock Tarn*, so-called for its water lilies. Rock shelves part way along the western bank make a good picnic spot.

From the tarn we trend northward and soon get a first sight of *Watendlath*, a sheet of dark water with the whitewashed farm on its far shore. Descending the moor we eventually enter a farm lane that leads to a ford and picturesque stone footbridge at the outflow.

The return is more direct, on a well-used bridleway from the footbridge heading south-west over *Puddingstone Bank* and down to *Rosthwaite* in under an hour.

DOCK TARN & WATENDLATH

DISTANCE: 9KM/5.5MILES » **TOTAL ASCENT:** 435M/1,427FT » **START GR:** NY 258149 » **TIME:** ALLOW 4 HOURS **MAP:** OS EXPLORER OL4, THE ENGLISH LAKES NORTH-WESTERN AREA, 1:25,000 » **REFRESHMENTS:** TEA ROOMS AT ROSTHWAITE AND WATENDLATH, PUBS AT ROSTHWAITE AND STONETHWAITE » **NAVIGATION:** STRAIGHTFORWARD, HOWEVER ATTENTION NEEDED WHEN BRANCHING OFF THE CUMBRIA WAY TO ASCEND INTO OAK WOODS BY WILLYGRASS GILL.

Directions — Dock Tarn & Watendlath

➏ Rosthwaite, Borrowdale. From the north end of the village, take tarmac lane east (opposite bus shelter) signposted *PB Stonethwaite 1 mile, Watendlath 1.5 miles*. Cross bridge over Stonethwaite Beck.

2 **Turn right** immediately over bridge, signposted *Stonethwaite 1 mile*. At junction with Stonethwaite Bridge (after 1 mile) continue **straight ahead**, signposted *Grasmere via Greenup Edge*.

3 10mins after Stonethwaite Bridge, a stone **sheepfold** is reached. **Branch left** off the main path, to pass uphill side of sheepfold and follow grassy path angling SE uphill (through bracken in summer). Cross stone stile in wall and shortly afterwards a wooden stile as path enters oak wood. Ascend steeply on engineered path through wood.

4 Lingy End. Path leaves top of the wood and reaches a fine viewpoint by a small ruin. Continue over hummocky moor, crossing one stile, to Dock Tarn.

5 Skirt **west side** of tarn (good picnic rocks part way along) and follow only path, winding northward; Watendlath Tarn comes into view, descend to kissing gate and over stream. Curve around hillside and over boggy ground (stone slabs) to minor junction.

6 **Turn right**, descending gently, eastwards at first, curving around slope to kissing gate and on to ford stream, through a gate to a farm lane that leads to the north end of Watendlath Tarn and stone footbridge over to farm and tea room.

7 Return over footbridge and follow broad bridleway, signposted *Rosthwaite* over the watershed at Puddingstone Bank, descending easily to point **2** at Rosthwaite Bridge. Cross over to village.

05 DOCK TARN & WATENDLATH

BEAUTIFUL BORROWDALE; THE WEST FLANK OF CASTLE CRAG

06 Cat Bells – High Spy – Dale Head 20km/12miles

A round of contrasts; sheltered Borrowdale, a pocket peak and a fell top promenade.

Grange » Manesty » Cat Bells » Maiden Moor » High Spy » Dale Head (753m) » Honister Hause »
Tongue Gill » Broadslack Gill » Hollows Farm campsite » Grange

Start

Bridge over the River Derwent at Grange. Parking by side of B5289 Borrowdale road 300m north of bridge. Bus stop (from Keswick) by bridge.
GR: NY 254175.

The Walk

Cat Bells, perfectly poised between Derwent Water and the Newlands valley, is justly popular; a mountain in miniature. But don't be misled by its Beatrix Potter associations into thinking this is going to be an easy day. Cat Bells, for this outing, is just a stepping stone to higher peaks and one of the longest rounds in the book (unless you take the shortcuts).

For the first 3.5km it is very easy going, taking the lane from *Grange* to *Manesty* where we follow the contouring line of the Allerdale Ramble north to the foot of *Cat Bells* ascended by a fine ridge. From the cairn-less top we can gaze down on the chimney pots of whitewashed Little Town – a scene straight out of Potter's *The Tale of Mrs Tiggy-Winkle*.

Beyond Cat Bells, the walk assumes a more robust character as the moor top miles stretch south to *High Spy* and down to *Dalehead Tarn*. The well-made cairn on High Spy stands above a dramatic band of crags on the Newlands side, though these are best appreciated as we zigzag up the west flank of *Dale Head*. The fell's name says it all; its summit cairn tall above the crag's rim looking straight down the trench of Newlands.

Descending south, we get a good view across to Honister Crag, pocked with tunnel mouths and the haulage ways of the slate mines. Nearing the mine buildings on *Honister Hause*, we turn eastwards to pick up a bridleway that swings northward, carrying us around to Tongue Gill and on below the pines of Castle Crag in the 'Jaws of Borrowdale'. Soon we reach the River Derwent, a farm track and lanes leading back to Grange.

CAT BELLS – HIGH SPY – DALE HEAD

DISTANCE: 20KM/12MILES **» TOTAL ASCENT:** 1,200M/3,937FT **» START GR:** NY 254175 **» TIME:** ALLOW 7.5 HOURS **MAP:** OS EXPLORER OL4, THE ENGLISH LAKES NORTH-WESTERN AREA, 1:25,000 **» REFRESHMENTS:** TWO TEAROOMS AT GRANGE **» NAVIGATION:** CARE NEEDED IN POOR VISIBILITY ON CREST OF MAIDEN MOOR AND HIGH SPY, POSSIBLE MAP AND COMPASS WORK. OTHERWISE NO PROBLEMS, MANY OBVIOUS FEATURES.

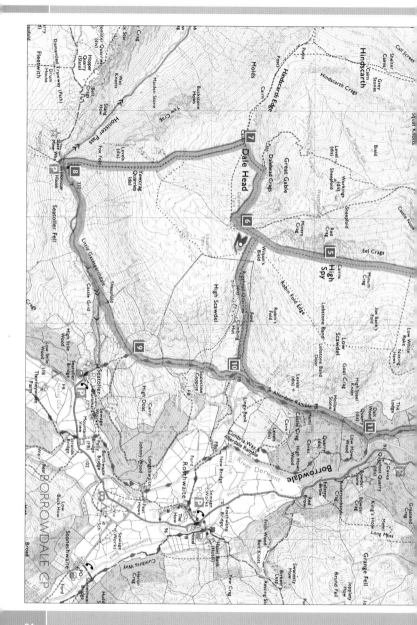

06 CAT BELLS – HIGH SPY – DALE HEAD

Directions – Cat Bells – High Spy – Dale Head

1 From the bridge at Grange, follow road through village, pass Borrowdale Gates Hotel on right and on to *Manesty*, 1.5km from bridge.

2 Manesty, farm-turned-holiday cottages on brow. Leave road, **branching left** on path that contours briefly then angles up hillside from gate and stile. In 5mins **fork right** towards top corner of wood*. Follow path – part of the Allerdale Ramble – for 2.5km, contouring north, passing Walpole memorial plaque by viewpoint bench and touching the fellside road at small quarry/parking bay before rising left.

*SC: Left fork heads up to Hause Gate and cuts out Cat Bells, shortening route by 4km and 85m of ascent.

3 Just as path is about to join the road a second time, **turn left**, steeply up to join main Cat Bells path – ascending generally SW up the nose of the fell, via several rock steps, **possibly slippery**.

4 **Cat Bells** (451m). From summit descend south to Hause Gate saddle (path crossing), continuing ahead up broad, and somewhat braided path, veering SW on to Maiden Moor (576m). At Bull Crag path curves south and holds this general line, undulating along the fell top for 2km towards High Spy.

5 **High Spy** (653m), cairn on summit overlooking Newlands valley. Descend south, steeply in places, and gradually veering SW. Dalehead Tarn comes into view*.

*SC: Descent to Grange via Rigghead quarries, **cutting out Dale Head**, shortening route by 5km and 283m of ascent. As tarn comes into view, branch left across fellside to fence above quarries. No clear path, just indistinct lines avoiding boggy ground in the saddle between Dalehead Tarn and fence. Stiles over fence, then clear path descending through former mine workings and beside beck to instruction **10**.)

6 Cross beck and skirt north side of Dalehead Tarn. Ascend westwards, some zigzags.

7 **Dale Head** (753m). Pillar-like cairn on summit comes into close view as plateau is breasted. **Descend southwards**. Slim iron fence post a few metres from summit cairn is a good guide to direction off flattish top. More heaped cairns soon appear. Part way down (c600m) fence on right bounds Yewdale quarries. Keep on left side of fence.

8 Honister Hause. At road **turn left**, pass youth hostel and bus stop, and follow road a short distance. **Bear left** on track descending eastwards, rejoining the road for c70m, then **bearing left again**, marked *Bridleway* on slate sign. Through gate, track swings northwards.

9 **Bear left** on track signed *Public Bridleway Grange* and also *Bridleway* on slate. Soon through gate in wall and **straight ahead** with wall on right. Northwards through gates and over footbridges to gate and bridge at Tongue Gill.

10 **Cross bridge** and continue northwards on bridleway to descend beneath west flank of Castle Crag, through gate into woodland, footbridges over Broadslack Gill beck.

11 As beck meets River Derwent, **bear left**, and on to pass vehicle barrier and join farm track. Northwards, soon passing Hollows Farm campsite, to emerge at a tarmac lane. **Turn right** and follow lane into Grange village.

CAT BELLS FROM MAIDEN MOOR

SECTION 2

East

Ullswater, for many the loveliest lake in England, lies at the heart of this section. The Roman 'High Street' marches to its east along the long broad spine of that name, while the Helvellyn range rises to the west. There is a good chance of seeing red deer on the less-frequented path over Beda Fell or from Rest Dodd. And on the more demanding Helvellyn side there is the challenge of the scramble along the serrated rocks of Striding Edge.

CALM OVER SHARROW BAY ULLSWATER. TAKEN EN ROUTE TO MARTINDALE (WALK 7)

HELVELLYN SUMMIT WINTER (WALK 10)

BEDA FELL & PLACE FELL

DISTANCE: 11KM/6.8 MILES » **TOTAL ASCENT:** 770M/2,526FT » **START GR:** NY 434184 » **TIME:** ALLOW 5.5 HOURS
MAP: OS EXPLORER OL5 THE ENGLISH LAKES, NORTH-EASTERN AREA, 1:25000 » **REFRESHMENTS:** NONE ON ROUTE.
NEAREST, HOWTOWN HOTEL » **NAVIGATION:** CARE NEEDED TO CHECK THE RIGHT LINE OFF PLACE FELL (5) NE OVER HART
CRAG AND ALSO THE SHARP RIGHT DESCENT AT 7.

PLACE FELL SUMMIT

07 Beda Fell & Place Fell

A less trodden fell top round on the quiet side of Ullswater.

Martindale Old Church » Howsteadbrow » Beda Fell » Boredale Hause » Place Fell (657m) » Low Moss » Garth Heads » Martindale Old Church

Start

Park by the green at Martindale Old Church on the lane leading along Howe Grain. Approached on lane down east side of Ullswater from Pooley Bridge, 8km/5 miles. GR: NY 434184.

The Walk

Place Fell's craggy west flank rises abruptly above the southern end of Ullswater, the fell as a whole having a commanding presence that belies its relatively modest height. The standard approach is from Patterdale but we have chosen the grassy ridges enclosing the quiet valley of *Boredale*. *Martindale Old Church* at the start repays a short investigation. Overshadowing the northern end of the atmospheric building is a large yew said to be up to 2,000 years old while inside is a baptismal font once part of a Roman shrine on High Street.

Leaving the tarmac at *Winter Crag Farm*, we head up a bracken slope to *Howsteadbrow* where a wrought iron bench looks to Sandwick Bay and Ullswater. Turning south we begin an agreeable ascent of the long ridge of *Beda Fell*. It's easy going, with a possibility of sighting red deer that reside on The Nab, lying to our east.

From *Bedafell Knott* we descend to the broad col of Boredale Hause. Other walkers will probably appear, coming up from Patterdale. The ruin that looks like a tumbled sheepfold but bears the title *'Chapel in the House'* on the OS map was indeed a place of prayer centuries ago, rumoured to have been built by St Patrick.

A more recent 'construction' here is the pathway that winds up Place Fell's south flank. It deposits us at the foot of a short eroded gully that leads to a false summit and then along a flattish ridge top to a rocky knobble surmounted by a trig' point (657m). It's a fine vantage point, with St Sunday Crag and the Helvellyn range marching to our west.

We descend NW past pools fringed with cotton grass, then more steeply from *Hart Crag*, across open moorland, and eventually down to the lane at *Garth Head*. Just when you could do without it, there is now the short, sharp shock of 80 metres uphill to *Howsteadbrow*, where the bench is a welcome spot to drain one's flask before descending to the Old Church.

Directions – Beda Fell & Place Fell

➔ From Martindale Old Church follow lane SW over bridge by Winter Crag Farm. At farm entrance grassy path (bracken fringed in summer) heads uphill towards broken crags, angles rightwards with stonewall on right, then away from wall towards skyline, reached c20mins from church.

2 Howsteadbrow. Skyline reached at an iron bench looking towards Ullswater. **Turn left** (S) to ascend ridge. Pleasant grassy path, occasional rocky steps, gaining height steadily to Beda Head (509m), dipping to broad saddle and then climbing again to Bedafell Knott (500m).

3 Path junction with small pile of stones, just south of Bedafell Knott (3km or approx 1hour 30mins from iron bench). Old bridleway rises from Bannerdale side and crosses en route to Patterdale. **Turn right** on this, heading SW round hillside and then down towards Boredale Hause. After Freeze Beck path swings westwards and braids. Aim for ruin of 'Chapel in the Hause' and the foot of the obvious path up Place Fell.

4 **Boredale Hause** (399m). From 'chapel' take engineered footpath curving up south flank of Place Fell. Summit plateau gained by short eroded gully at Round How. Broad ridge with small pools follows to rocky knoll topped by trig' point.

5 **Place Fell** (657m). Descend from summit knoll and **aim NE along broad ridge**, passing small tarn on its left side and on to the knobble of Hart Crag. Path now descends, more steeply at first, still NE, towards an abandoned sheepfold on the saddle of Low Moss.

6 Path forks at sheepfold. **Take right-hand branch**, still heading NE, rising slightly at first, around eastern shoulder of High Dodd. Good grassy track contouring around hillside.

7 As High Dodd is passed, about 15mins from sheepfold, **turn right** on overgrown path (in summer) dropping abruptly E towards Boredale. Path soon swings leftwards and angles steadily down. Above a small stone barn **double back right** and follow path to stile and over boggy field to clapstone footbridge over Boredale Beck.

8 Garth Heads. From footbridge join farm track, by ford, and follow this, stile by gate, to lane. **Straight across**, barn on left, and over another stile, to ascend to the iron bench, first met at **2**, and follow the outward route back to the church.

07 BEDA FELL & PLACE FELL

LOOKING ACROSS HAWESWATER TO RIGGINDALE EDGE (LINE OF ROUTE)

08 High Street from Mardale Head 11.25km/7miles

Superb stairway ridge to the High Street of Romans and feasting shepherds.

Mardale Head » The Rigg » Rough Crag » Long Stile » High Street (828m) » Mardale Ill Bell » Nan Bield Pass » Harter Fell » Gatescarth Pass » Mardale Head

Start

Small car park at Mardale Head, the end of the tarmac road at southern end of Haweswater reservoir. GR: NY 469107.

The Walk

High Street boasts no soaring eminence but its east face is wonderfully savage; dark crags above wind-rippled Blea Water. It sounds forbidding, yet on this approach we can appreciate the setting from a 3km ridge that forms one of the finest natural stairways in the Lake District.

From *Mardale Head* we circle the southern end of Haweswater to gain the ridge just above The Rigg, a wooded headland jutting into the reservoir. Beneath the waters are the remains of Mardale Green, inundated in the 1930s to slake the thirsts of Manchester. Ascending the ridge, the path is obvious, either on the broad crest or slightly left, negotiating occasional rocky steps. Below to the north, and mainly out of sight, is a series of broken crags, including Eagle Crag, a reminder that Riggindale is (or sadly 'was') home to the last breeding golden eagles in England.

After the grandeur of the ridge, *High Street's* summit plateau is an anti-climax – flat and often waterlogged. Yet it is steeped in history. Roman soldiers marched along its length between forts at Ambleside and Penrith and up to the 19th century shepherds would gather here every July to exchange stock, race horses, feast on ale and cake and pit cousin against cousin in Cumberland wrestling.

Finding the correct line southeast to *Mardale Ill Bell* has been made easier with a new raised path across boggy ground and we're soon dropping to the *Nan Bield Pass*, once a busy route between Kendal and Penrith. For the weary it also provides a shortcut back to Mardale Head. Our final ascent is over *Harter Fell* where the summit cairn sprouts a sculpture of rusted iron fence posts. The grassy top affords a fine view north across Haweswater, to which we now return via *Gatesgarth Pass*.

HIGH STREET FROM MARDALE HEAD

DISTANCE: 11.25KM/7MILES » **TOTAL ASCENT:** 850M/2,789FT » **START GR:** NY 469107 » **TIME:** ALLOW 5.5 HOURS
MAP: OS EXPLORER OL5 THE ENGLISH LAKES, NORTH-EASTERN AREA, 1:25,000 » **REFRESHMENTS:** NONE. NEAREST, HAWESWATER HOTEL » **NAVIGATION:** THE LONG SUMMIT OF HIGH STREET IS FLAT AND FEATURELESS SAVE FOR THE STONE WALL THAT RUNS N-S ALONG ITS LENGTH. THIS IS A VITAL GUIDE IN POOR VISIBILITY. EVEN SO, IN CLOUD, MAP AND COMPASS WORK MAY BE NEEDED TO LOCATE WALL AFTER REACHING THE SUMMIT PLATEAU AND FOR AIMING OFF TO MARDALE ILL BELL. OTHERWISE THE PATHS ARE CLEAR.

HIGH STREET SUMMIT WALL

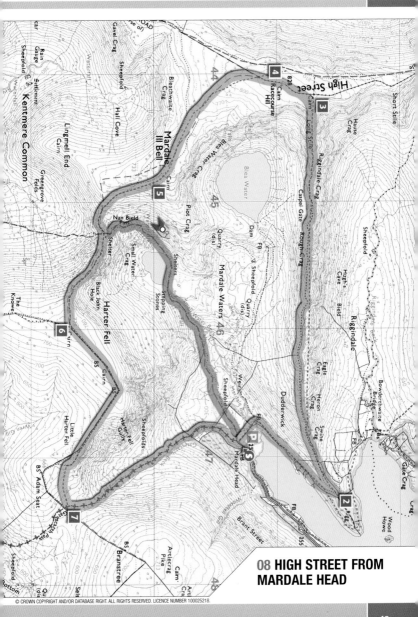

08 HIGH STREET FROM MARDALE HEAD

Directions – High Street from Mardale Head

8 Through the gate at the end of the car park onto the Gatescarth Pass track for just a few yards before **turning right** at corner of the stone wall and following path rightwards around the head of the reservoir, crossing Mardale Beck. Path heads NE, after 500m bears uphill away from reservoir, plantation on right, to brow of The Rigg.

2 Through opening in wall (view into Riggindale) **turn left** up ridge. In 10mins path cuts through gap in wall to cairn and begins steeper climb, at first on left of ridge. After crossing Rough Crag the path dips to a saddle, Caspel Gate, with a small tarn, then climbs to a cairn on the edge of the summit plateau.

3 From cairn, **head SW to wall**, not visible at first. Wall runs N-S the length of High Street. Follow wall south to summit trig' point (828m) – barely 10mins walk from cairn at plateau edge.

4 **High Street** (828m). From trig' point, follow wall south for 300m (5mins), **bear left** on engineered path over boggy ground, looping round to head SE to Mardale III Bell.

5 **Mardale III Bell** (760m). **Descend SE**, path cobbled in parts, to solid windbreak on Nan Bield Pass and path crossroads*. **Ascend ESE** to cairn on brow of Harter Fell and on in 2mins to summit.

⟳ ***SC**: From Nan Bield windbreak descend north to Small Water and on to Mardale Head.

6 **Harter Fell** (778m). Rusted iron fence posts embedded in cairn. From summit, **head NE**, keeping chain-link fence on right, to cairn and then viewpoint at north end of fell top. Engineered path descends SE, at first by fence side, then curving east to join Gatescarth Pass track just north of gate on pass.

7 Descend on track northwards for 1.5km to car park at Mardale Head.

ANGLE TARN & REST DODD

DISTANCE: 11KM/7MILES » **TOTAL ASCENT:** 710M/2,329FT » **START GR:** NY 410130 » **TIME:** ALLOW 4.5 HOURS
MAP: OS EXPLORER OL5 THE ENGLISH LAKES, NORTH-EASTERN AREA, 1:25,000 » **REFRESHMENTS:** NONE ON ROUTE.
NEAREST PUB BROTHERSWATER INN ON A592 AT KIRKSTONEFOOT. PUBS AND CAFÉS IN PATTERDALE AND GLENRIDDING
NAVIGATION: PATH INDISTINCT ON SLOPES OF REST DODD; IN MIST, MAP AND COMPASS SKILLS MAY BE REQUIRED.
ELSEWHERE CLEAR PATHS AND TRACKS.

ABOVE ANGLE TARN EN ROUTE TO REST DODD

09 Angle Tarn & Rest Dodd

11km/7miles

On the Eastern Fells by a lovely tarn in the realm of red deer.

Hartsop » Boredale Hause » Angle Tarn » Satura Crag » Rest Dodd (696m) » Hayeswater » Hartsop

Start

Car park at the end of lane through hamlet of Hartsop, 500m east off A592 Patterdale–Kirkstone Pass road just north of Brothers Water. GR: NY 410130.

The Walk

Angle Tarn is a rightly popular destination. Unlike many Lakeland tarns, it doesn't hide in the shadow of a deep cwm, but spreads irregularly about a shallow hollow just below the ridge running from Boredale Hause towards High Street. We visit the tarn in a round that also takes in the grassy dome of Rest Dodd in a less frequented area where there is a good chance of seeing red deer.

The walk starts *through* the hamlet of *Hartsop*. It would be easy to bypass it, but a shame, because Hartsop possesses an unfussy charm, its 17th century cottages and barns still much the same as impressed Wordsworth 200 years ago. Special vernacular features include stepped gables, circular chimneys and spinning galleries. There's even a green painted oven set in a wall.

From the foot of Hartsop we follow a bridleway north on the valley floor before ascending the fellside to *Boredale Hause*. Here we join the Coast to Coast route and turn south to *Angle Tarn*. If time and good visibility allows, it is worth scrambling up to the twin tops of *Angletarn Pikes*. Only the southeast top gives a view over the tarn – and it is two metres lower than its neighbour. 'Baggers', therefore, may need to visit both.

At *Satura Crag* we turn away from the main track and ascend the broad east shoulder of *Rest Dodd*. There's not much of path but the turf is a treat underfoot. Look out for red deer whose sanctuary is The Nab, the promontory hill directly north of Rest Dodd. The herd is indigenous – a rarity for red deer in England – and groups wander widely over the fells between Ullswater and High Street.

We descend to *Hayeswater*, which provides drinking water for Penrith, and follow a good track from the reservoir outflow down to *Hartsop*. It's an agreeable end to the day; easy walking, the beck cascading in its deep cleft, and part way down, the ruins of an old lead mine – a commercial failure that only briefly disturbed this lovely valley.

CLOUD SEA LAPS FELLS, LOOKING NE FROM REST DODD

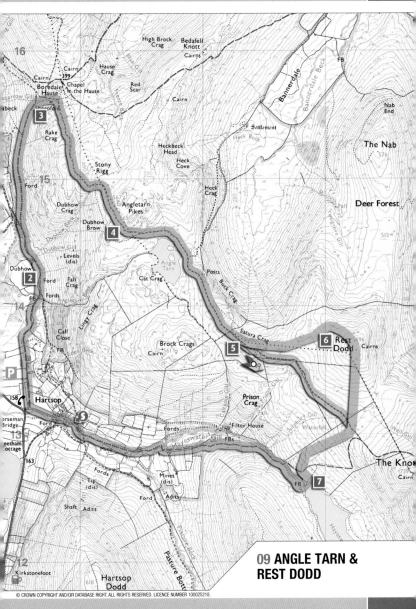

09 ANGLE TARN & REST DODD

Directions – Angle Tarn & Rest Dodd

➊ From Hartsop car park walk back down the lane through the hamlet and almost to the A592 main road. Just before this **turn right** at white house/outdoor centre into tarmac lane. At entrance to Hartsop Fold holiday chalets continue **straight ahead** on bridleway between stone walls.

2 Pass through gate and over footbridge over Angletarn Beck. Open fell now on right. About 500m after footbridge **fork right** on good track (bridleway) angling up the fellside. Continue ascending steadily to Boredale Hause.

3 Boredale Hause. After crossing Stonebarrow Gill, track is joined by another coming up from Patterdale. This is Boredale Hause. Low cairn and manhole cover on flat area. **Turn right** to recross Stonebarrow Gill just above a ruined sheepfold. Path has a few stone steps just after the beck and then climbs steadily, heading SSE.

4 Path curves around the shoulder of Angletarn Pikes and descends gently eastwards to skirt the east side of the tarn. From the tarn, continue on same path, rising SSE.

Angletarn Pikes *repay a visit as an excellent viewpoint. There are two pikes of which the northern is marginally the higher – by two metres. Leave the path just before the shoulder where a faint grassy trail leads to the top (567m). Return the same way or cross to the southern pike and descend from there to the tarn (several faint trails). The pair add 60m of ascent to the day.*

5 Some 700m from Angle Tarn, path meets a wall, passes between stout gateposts and continues, wall to right hand, along ridge with Bannerdale to left and Hayeswater to the right. After passing above Satura Crag, as path braids among boulders, **veer left** away from wall and cross dip to follow minor path rising eastward up broad shoulder of Rest Dodd*.

➋ *SC: Rest Dodd could be omitted by following the path that continues alongside the wall and picking up the descent path to Hayeswater described in instruction **6**.

6 **Rest Dodd** (696m). Follow grassy path up shoulder to summit. From the second (main) cairn, leave southwards and descend to wall corner. Continue south down fellside to wall coming straight up from valley and **descend SW to Hayeswater outflow** with wall away to right hand. Path occasionally indistinct.

7 **Cross footbridge** at Hayeswater outflow and **turn right** to follow good track easily down for 2km to Hartsop car park, crossing Hayeswater beck halfway down.

FROSTED CAIRN, RAKE CRAG ABOVE BOREDALE HAUSE

HELVELLYN & RAISE VIA STRIDING EDGE

DISTANCE: 16KM/10MILES » **TOTAL ASCENT:** 1,050M/3,445FT » **START GR:** NY 386169 » **TIME:** ALLOW 7 HOURS **MAP:** OS EXPLORER OL5 THE ENGLISH LAKES, NORTH-EASTERN AREA, 1:25,000 » **REFRESHMENTS:** FELLBITES CAFÉ BESIDE CAR PARK; TRAVELLERS REST PUB, GLENRIDDING » **NAVIGATION:** SEVERAL ROUTES RADIATE FROM GLENRIDDING, HEAD FOR 'HELVELLYN VIA MIRESBECK'. SUMMIT PLATEAU FEATURELESS IN MIST, MAP AND COMPASS SKILLS MAY BE REQUIRED. **BE AWARE:** STRIDING EDGE IS A ROCK SCRAMBLE. IT IS NOT TECHNICALLY DIFFICULT BUT IT IS EXPOSED. POLISHED ROCK CAN BE SLIPPERY WHEN WET. UNDER SNOW OR ICE, IT SHOULD NOT BE ATTEMPTED UNLESS COMPETENT IN THE USE OF ICE AXE AND CRAMPONS.

TRAVERSING STRIDING EDGE, HELVELLYN AHEAD

10 Helvellyn & Raise via Striding Edge   16km/10miles

Exhilarating scramble followed by a high level walk along the roof of Lakeland.

Glenridding » Miresbeck » Birkhouse Moor » Striding Edge » Helvellyn (950m) » Whiteside Bank »
Raise » Sticks Pass » Greenside Mine » Glenridding

Start

LDNP pay and display in the centre of Glenridding village, by Ullswater.
GR: NY 386169.

The Walk

Helvellyn is deservedly one of the most popular mountains in England and its ascent by the scramble along the serrations of Striding Edge the most coveted. Yet, by the route described here, large parts of the day are enjoyed in relative solitude.

Leaving the village, passing the *Travellers Rest* pub, we cross Glenridding Beck and soon begin a steady ascent of the coomb enclosing *Mires Beck*, turning westwards at its head onto *Birkhouse Moor*. A cairn just off the path at the northern crest of the moor affords a panorama of our skyline route for the day.

Easy strolling takes us past the *Hole-in-the-Wall* junction, where probably we will pick up company, and on to the day's *pièce de résistance – Striding Edge*. Except in slippery or winter conditions, it is not difficult, though it is literally 'hands on' in places. What impresses is the airy feel of the ridge

plunging away to either side. Wordsworth wrote of the "skeleton arms" extending from Helvellyn's trunk; Striding Edge is the most skeletal of all.

The ridge proper ends with the descent of a steep groove to a notch, but scrambling continues up the blunt prow to Helvellyn's plateau and soon the welcoming windbreak cairn – scene of a million packed lunches. Beyond the summit scalp of stones lies 4km of fell top highway, undulating over *Whiteside* and Raise to the broad saddle of *Sticks Pass*.

East from the pass the character changes, a more intimate path above *Sticks Gill* beck, skirting a marsh and mine spoil heaps before descending to buildings at *Greenside* road-head. Around us are the remains of Greenside Lead Mine that operated for 200 years before being abandoned in 1962. A 2km stroll down Greenside Road returns us to *Glenridding*.

STRIDING EDGE; HANDS ON

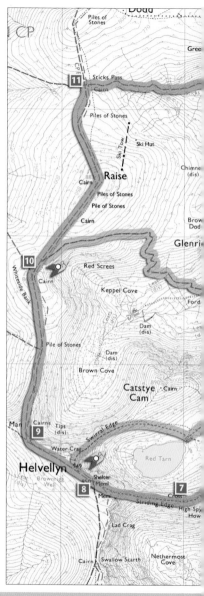

**10 HELVELLYN & RAISE
VIA STRIDING EDGE**

Directions – Helvellyn & Raise via Striding Edge

➊ Leave Glenridding car park by exit in its NW corner, by small health centre, and follow lane of cottages west, passing **Travellers Rest pub**.

2 At top of village, 100m past the pub, **turn left** down lane signed *Gillside Farm*. Cross Rattlebeck Bridge with caravan park on right. Approaching end of the tarmac, **bear right** on track with stonewall on right. At junction continue uphill through gate, signposted *PF Helvellyn via Miresbeck 3 miles*. At walled wood bear right heading to ladder stile and gate.

3 Through gate **immediately turn left**, soon crossing Mires Beck and ascending coomb.

4 Large pile of stones as skyline is reached, ruined sheepfold on right. **Bear right**, uphill, on path beside wall. After c10mins **veer right**, away from wall, on path angling up hillside.

5 Birkhouse Moor. Path curves westward as moor top is reached. Viewpoint cairn is just out of sight about 50m right of path. Check this out and resume easy walking SW, soon with wall on left.

6 Hole-in-the-Wall. Path crossroads. **Continue ahead**. (Path on left is rising from Grisedale, that on right from Red Tarn).

7 Striding Edge scramble begins at a rocky knoll. The way is well worn, keeping on or close to the ridgeline. **Much of the scrambling can be bypassed** by a path slightly lower on the Red Tarn side. Beyond notch, as the rock gives way to scree and grass, trend rightwards. Soon Helvellyn summit windbreak comes into view.

8 **Helvellyn** (950m). From windbreak, cross stony summit to a trig' point and then to a cairn marking the descent to Swirral Edge*. **Bear left** at cairn on broad felltop path.

> **⊘ *SC**: Descending via Swirral Edge and Red Tarn Beck path to instruction **12** shortens the route by 2.5km/1.5 miles. **Take care**; loose and steep. Ice axe and crampons in snow/ice.

9 Path forks in a dip, about half a mile after leaving Helvellyn summit. **Bear right**, heading north over the brow of Lower Man, descending to a saddle then ascending again.

10 **Whiteside Bank** (863m). Soon after leaving cairn and windbreak top, path forks in a dip*. **Bear left** up **Raise** (883m) topped by a well-made cairn. Descend north to broad saddle.

> *SC: Bearing right and descending to instruction **12** would shorten the route by 1.25km/0.75 miles.

11 Sticks Pass. Path crossing marked by low cairn. **Turn right**, descending eastwards. After 1.5km path swings southwards around end of marsh and by mine spoil heaps; sporadic cairns. Cross beck on wooden bridge. Cairns lead to old mine track winding down to Greenside buildings.

12 A couple of waymark posts indicate final line of descent to buildings, but it is obvious. Through gate and over bridge of Swart Beck on to lane, Youth Hostel on right. Follow Greenside Road 2km to Glenridding, rejoining outward route just before the Travellers Rest pub. Thirsty?

RED TARN FROM HELVELLYN

DOVE CRAG & LITTLE HART CRAG

DISTANCE: 12.5KM/8MILES » **TOTAL ASCENT:** 866M/2,841FT » **START GR:** NY 403134 » **TIME:** ALLOW 4.5–5 HOURS
MAP: OS EXPLORER OL5 THE ENGLISH LAKES, NORTH-EASTERN AREA, 1:25,000 » **REFRESHMENTS:** BROTHERSWATER INN
ON A592 AT KIRKSTONEFOOT » **NAVIGATION:** PATHS AND TRACKS THROUGHOUT, HOWEVER MAP AND COMPASS WORK
MAY BE NEEDED ON HIGH GROUND BETWEEN SCANDALE PASS AND DOVE CRAG IN POOR VISIBILITY, PARTICULARLY IF SNOW
OBSCURES PATHS.

11 **Dove Crag & Little Hart Crag** 12.5km/8miles

Fell top hike above the crags and woods of beautiful Dovedale.

Cow Bridge (Patterdale) » Hartsop Hall » Caiston Glen » Scandale Pass » Little Hart Crag » Dove Crag (792m) » Dovedale » Hartsop Hall » Cow Bridge

Start

Cow Bridge car park on A592 near Hartsop hamlet, 3km south of Patterdale village. GR: NY 403134.

The Walk

Dove Crag lies midway on the bulky mountain chain between Fairfield and Red Screes above Kirkstone Pass. Wild and precipitous on its complex east face, by contrast, on the west side grassy slopes dip away to the valley of Rydal Beck. Strictly speaking the name Dove Crag does not apply to the hilltop itself but to the dark cliff looming at the head of Dovedale. Overhanging in places, and respected by rock climbers for its high-grade routes, we get a close look at Dove Crag as we descend from the fell top.

From the car park at *Cow Bridge* a good track leads pleasantly by Goldrill Beck and past Brothers Water to *Hartsop Hall Farm* – an architecturally fascinating building dating back to the 15th century, now owned by the National Trust. Bearing south across meadows, one dotted with boulders like standing stones, we enter quiet *Caiston Glen* for a steady ascent above the beck to the skyline at *Scandale Pass*.

We're now on the undulating fell top with the rocky eminence of *Little Hart Crag* standing proud to the north. From the cairn on the westerly of its twin tops, reached by a short easy scramble, we get a good idea of the route ahead, skirting Bakestones Moss, then swinging north up a broad ridge. *Note the energetic alternative route up Little Hart Crag, given in instruction 4.*

The summit cairn for *Dove Crag* (792m) is easily missed in poor weather, standing a little to the east of the tumbled wall that is our guide over the fell. For the curious, the rim of the crag itself lies some 300m NNW of the cairn. We follow the wall down to the col rising to Hart Crag and turn east on a cairned scar swinging rightwards to below Dove Crag. This is rough terrain and care must be exercised as we descend a steep gully (some steps), passing below a ruined building, to *Dovedale Beck*. Above the main crag is Priest's Hole, which was once a lonely retreat. More recently it has served as a shelter for climbers.

A good path traverses the north slope of the valley, through woods and past the remains of *Hartsop Hall lead mine* – worked sporadically from at least the 17th century until abandonment in 1942. At the farm we rejoin our outward route.

DOVE CRAG

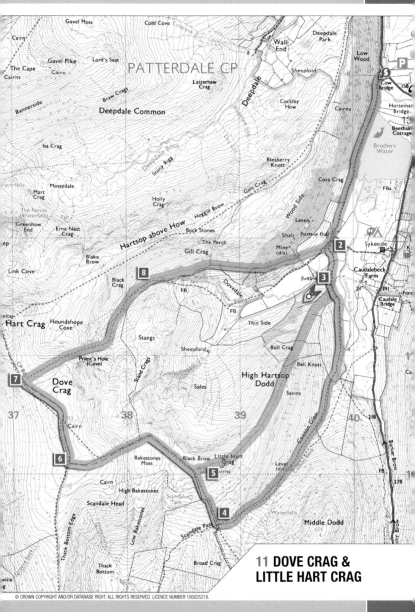

**11 DOVE CRAG &
LITTLE HART CRAG**

Directions – Dove Crag & Little Hart Crag

↪ From Cow Bridge car park, go through gate on west side of bridge over Goldrill Beck (PF signpost). Head south on track by beck and Brothers Water to Hartsop Hall farm.

2 Hartsop Hall. Pass rear of hall on track heading to farm sheds. Before reaching these **branch left** over small footbridge, signed *FP to Kirkstone Pass and Scandale Pass*, and through gate in stone wall. **Turn right** as indicated by yellow arrows on posts, to sheds, **then left** across field on grassy track to wooden bridge. Continue on track over field by large boulder.

3 Through gate by stone barn. **Choice of routes** to Little Hart Crag. For route via **Scandale Pass** continue southwards in valley bottom with wall on left. After about 500m wall dips away left to Kirkstone Beck. Path continues south, gradually swinging rightwards and ascending towards Caiston Glen. Pass through gates at sheepfold and continue up glen with beck below to left.

▷OR▷ from 3: From stone barn, **bear right** and ascend SW **directly up nose** of fell on worn path. Strenuous. Angle eases at knoll of High Hartsop Dodd and grassy path continues to summit rocks of Little Hart Crag. Rejoin main route at instruction **5**.

4 Scandale Pass. Broad col at 514m, small cairn and ladder stile over stone wall. Do not cross. **Turn right** just before wall and follow path north for 500m to junction just below Little Hart Crag, **turn right** and ascend on rocky path to summit.

5 **Little Hart Crag** (637m). From summit descend westwards to junction (already encountered by Scandale Pass route). Route now follows line of old fence posts, first NW then SW.

6 Junction with Dove Crag–High Pike path. (Grid Ref: NY 375101.) Fence posts meet wall here. **Turn right** and head north 400m to Dove Crag summit cairn (792m). This corner can be shortcut in good visibility. Descend northwards, wall on left.

7 At col between Dove Crag and Hart Crag, **turn right** and descend towards Dovedale. Path, cairned at first, swings beneath crag and descends steeply in gully on partly-cobbled 'stair', ruined building on left. Angle eases and path continues pleasantly with beck below on right.

8 **Remain on left bank** ignoring gate on far side of stream where another path descends via waterfall to valley bottom. Our path traverses fellside to a wall enclosing a wood and descends gently on the uphill side of the wall, finally across pasture to Hartsop Hall at instruction **2**. Follow outward track back to Cow Bridge car park.

WINTER OVER BROTHERS WATER

SECTION 3

South

This is the Lake District's gentler side, centred on Ambleside and Grasmere, and three of the walks in this section reflect that – those over Loughrigg, Lingmoor Fell and Blea Rigg. It is the Lakeland of Wordsworth, cascading becks and fells shaggy-coated with juniper and heather. On its western fringe though are two of the biggest walks in the book, a circuit of the Coniston fells and along the skyline of Crinkle Crags.

LOOKING OUT FROM SWIRL HOW, WETHERLAM BEYOND (WALK 16)

EASEDALE TARN AND VALE OF GRASMERE FROM BLEA RIGG (WALK 12)

BLEA RIGG FROM GRASMERE

DISTANCE: 12KM/7.5MILES » **TOTAL ASCENT:** 703M/2,306FT » **START GR:** NY 337076 » **TIME:** ALLOW 5 HOURS
MAPS: OS EXPLORER OL7 THE ENGLISH LAKES SOUTH-EASTERN AREA AND OL6 SOUTH-WESTERN AREA » **REFRESHMENTS:**
CAFÉS, RESTAURANTS AND PUBS GALORE IN GRASMERE » **NAVIGATION:** PATH BRAIDS OCCASIONALLY ALONG THE BROAD
RIDGE BETWEEN SILVER HOW AND BLEA RIGG WITH MINOR TRODS DIVERTING OFF, BUT MAIN LINE IS GENERALLY OBVIOUS.

LANGDALE PIKES AND PAVEY ARK (RIGHT) FROM BLEA RIGG

12 Blea Rigg from Grasmere

12km/7.5miles

Stride or stroll on a broad grassy ridge with a panorama of central Lakeland.

Grasmere » skyline above Chapel Stile » Swinescar Pike » Blea Rigg (541m) » Easedale Tarn » Grasmere

Start

Grasmere village green and bus stop, opposite the Heaton Cooper Studio. Pay and display car parks around village. GR: NY 337076.

The Walk

Blea Rigg, at 541m, is a modest fell both in height and appearance, yet rewards its visitors as the furthest point of a varied scenic round that can be undertaken in most weathers.

Turning our backs on the distractions of Grasmere – Wordsworth, Gingerbread and so on – we branch off the *Red Bank road* and up a good path towards *Silver How*. This is Lakeland at its most picturesque. We pass fine larches, seen over the wall to our left, as all the while the view of the lake and the vale of Grasmere expands. Higher up, the fell is decked with juniper.

Reaching the skyline, a valley of different character is revealed; Great Langdale, with Chapel Stile and its slate quarries almost at our feet. We've gained the crest of what is really a single broad finger of upland pointing from High Raise in the north-west to Windermere, at the Ambleside end.

From here we wend north-west, gaining height by modest degrees, the view alternating between Langdale on our left, with Pavey Ark and the Pikes splendidly arrayed, and Easedale on our right. It is easy going, passing a reed-fringed tarn, on to the diminutive cone of *Swinescar Pike*, and then to *Blea Rigg* itself. The summit cairn sits aside from the path on a rocky knuckle. Out of sight, though just a few steps further to the north, this seemingly benign fell drops away dramatically over Blea Crag.

After weaving over peat hags we gain a few more metres to a cairn that must be one of the best vantage points for the great rampart of Pavey Ark above Stickle Tarn. Soon we leave the ridge and descend into *Easedale*, a couple of stepped rocky slabs adding interest.

The tarn lies at the centre of a wide moorland bowl. De Quincey thought it 'the most gloomily sublime of all its class'. Cast with late afternoon sun the tarn is far from gloomy, and there is still the sparkle of the falls of *Sourmilk Gill* to come as we continue on a good track from the tarn's outflow all the way down to Grasmere.

DESCENDING TO EASEDALE

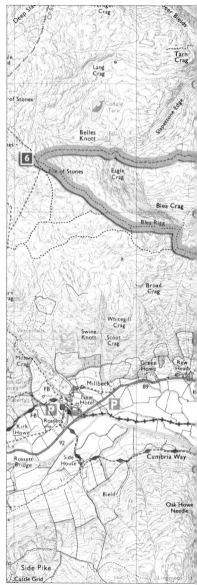

12 BLEA RIGG FROM GRASMERE

Directions – Blea Rigg from Grasmere

➎ From Grasmere village green take Langdale Road on right side of Grasmere Hotel. **Turn right** at T-junction, passing Red Bank car park on left. Follow road round bends.

2 **Leave road, turning right** through gate at PF sign opposite 'Faeryland Grasmere'. Good path ascending SW, first between stone walls, then across a grass field, and on towards fell, stone wall on left, craggy hillside on right. Several gates.

3 Path junction on brow, good view over Grasmere lake. Wall leaves us here, curving away leftwards. *For author's preferred route, **continue ahead** on path through bracken, crossing small streams, to large pile-of-stones cairn (**4**) on skyline overlooking Chapel Stile and quarry.

> **◄OR** *For Silver How option**, turn right at **3** and ascend steeply. Path leads to summit cairn. Leave on grassy path heading generally NW, passing above tarn to rejoin author's route just before **5**.

4 Skyline cairn (c287m). Path contours NW, crossing Megs Gill, up on to fell top and on past reedy tarn.

5 **Swinescar Pike** (410m). Conical mound to right of path, now reunited with Silver How traffic. Path meanders NW, passing small tarns and ascending crest of Blea Rigg. Summit cairn (541m) is on a rocky knoll, to right of path as one passes the more noticeable boulder-roofed 'shelter'. (**Note**: no summit spot height is shown on the OS map.) Beyond Blea Rigg, path braids around peat bog and ascends gradually. Cairn at c570 gives view to both Stickle Tarn to SW and Easedale Tarn to NE.

6 **Junction with path** crossing between Stickle Tarn/Langdale and Easedale Tarn/Grasmere. Somewhat indistinct with scattering of cairns. **Turn right**, eastwards, and descend steeply, zigzags and a couple of stepped slabs. Path from Codale Tarn joins from left. Continue down on right side of beck, path partially 'paved', angle easing as it heads to south side of tarn.

7   Easedale Tarn outflow. **Do not cross beck**. Remain on right-hand (south) side and descend on good path by cascades of Sourmilk Gill. Through gate and over field, **cross stream** on farm track and **bear left** through gate on partially cobbled track beside Easedale Beck. Through iron gate beneath trees and over footbridge onto Easedale Road. **Turn right** to village.

8   Permissive path behind hedge on right side of road, opposite houses, offers an off-road alternative route back into village, ending exactly at starting point. Easedale Road alternative joins village main street about 100m north of starting point.

GREAT LANGDALE SEEN FROM ABOVE CHAPEL STILE

13 Loughrigg Fell

10.5km/6.5miles

A gentle round in the footsteps of the Wordsworths.

Ambleside (Rydal Road car park) » Miller Bridge » Loughrigg Fell (335m) » Loughrigg Terrace »
Rydal Hall » Ambleside

Start

Ambleside's Rydal Road car park; large pay and display car park on A591 at north end of village. GR: NY 376047.

The Walk

Loughrigg is Ambleside's home fell and on any clear day you'll find, as well as visitors, several 'locals' up there reminding themselves why it is so good to live where they do. This round, over the fell top towards Grasmere and back via Rydal Hall, is the gentlest in this book but a pleasure all the way.

We start out by playing fields to cross the River Rothay by *Miller Bridge* – a packhorse bridge – and follow a bridleway, tarmac at first, past cottages and *Brow Head Farm*, and on to the fell at its southern end.

For a fell of such modest height, it can be confusing terrain. A criss-cross of paths has been created by countless folk wandering where the fancy takes them. The OS map also places the words 'Loughrigg Fell' some 300m south of the summit cairn.

We traverse the fell in a north-westerly direction, arriving first at a cairn on a rocky bluff overlooking Loughrigg Tarn. From here it's another undulating kilometre to the trig' point and cairn on the principal *summit (335m)* – an excellent place for a first-time visitor to get a sense of the geography of the surrounding high hills.

Descending NW, another expanse of water comes into view, Grasmere, and soon we are contouring above it on the popular *Loughrigg Terrace*, a favourite once of William and Dorothy Wordsworth. We pass by the vast (unsafe) cavern of Rydal quarry and down to the hamlet of *Rydal* itself – home of the Wordsworths from 1813 to 1850 and a place of pilgrimage from the age of the Romantics onwards.

The last leg takes us over Rydal Beck, at the rear of *Rydal Hall* (with a good tearoom in an outbuilding by the beck), leisurely across parkland to a pavement by the main A591, and so back into *Ambleside*.

LOUGHRIGG FELL

DISTANCE: 10.5KM/6.5MILES » **TOTAL ASCENT:** 420M/1,378FT » **START GR:** NY 376047 » **TIME:** ALLOW 4 HOURS
MAPS: OS EXPLORER OL7, THE ENGLISH LAKES SOUTH-EASTERN AREA, 1:25,000 » **REFRESHMENTS:** CAFÉS, RESTAURANTS AND PUBS GALORE IN AMBLESIDE. BADGER BAR AT RYDAL, TEAROOM AT RYDAL HALL AND COTE HOWE, NEAR RYDAL
FOOTBRIDGE » **NAVIGATION:** GOOD PATHS ALL THE WAY, THOUGH OCCASIONALLY BRAIDED OVER THE FELL TOP.

ABOVE RYDAL WATER

13 LOUGHRIGG FELL

Directions – Loughrigg Fell

❻ Leave Rydal Road car park, Ambleside, by vehicle entrance/bridge; **turn left**, pass fire and police stations and **turn left again** down Stoney Lane. At end, **turn right** on footpath signed *Miller Bridge*.

2 **Cross bridge** over River Rothay, **turn right** on lane, over cattle grid, and **turn left**, over another cattle grid, and up tarmac track, signed *Public Bridleway*. Wind uphill past cottages; tarmac ends, continue on bridleway passing Pine Rigg (house) and on to fell.

3 After almost 2km from **2**, ford stream to path junction and **turn right** up hillside. This junction is by a small tarn. Ascend to cairn on rocky bluff overlooking Loughrigg Tarn. Following cairned path undulating NW to fell summit.

4 **Loughrigg Fell summit** (335m), cairn and trig point. Descend on path NW with Grasmere straight ahead.

5 As path nears trees, **turn right** on balcony path called Loughrigg Terrace. At fork take **right-hand** path, briefly uphill, and continue balcony line.

6 At quarry-cave, **turn downhill**, passing another old quarry. Just before gate on track, **double-back left** towards lakeside (Rydal Water) and after a few metres **back right again** to enter woods through iron kissing gate just above lake. Through woods to exit by another kissing gate.

7 Rydal. Cross footbridge over River Rothay to A591 at Badger Bar pub. Cross road, **with care**, to pavement, **turn right** (towards Ambleside) and after 100m **turn left**, multiple signs, to pass Rydal Church.

8 About 150m up lane **turn right** to Rydal Hall, signed *PF Ambleside and The Old School Room Tea Shop*. Pass tea shop, over bridge, and between buildings, following signs, and on to broad track, southwards with woods on left, parkland on right.

9 At main road, cross to pavement, **turn left** and continue on pavement to Ambleside.

HEADING FOR LINGMOOR, CHAPEL STILE BELOW

14 Lingmoor Fell & Side Pike

12km/7.5miles

A Langdale round of mines, moor top and meadow.

Elterwater (Britannia Inn) » Elterwater quarry » Lingmoor Fell » Brown How (469m) » Side Pike » upper Gt Langdale » Chapel Stile » Elterwater

Start

Elterwater, by Britannia Inn. Parking on Elterwater Common.
GR: NY 328048.

The Walk

Ideally, this easy walk should be done in the bloom of late summer for the old name 'Lingmoor' translates as 'heather moor' and even in these over-grazed times it still holds true. The artist William Heaton Cooper thought it "a good place on which to laze away a summer day in the heather, listening to the hard-working bees and the distant waters of the Langdales".

We start out from *Elterwater* alongside Great Langdale Beck. On the opposite bank is the Langdale timeshare complex built on the site of the former Elterwater Gunpowder Works. You can still hear explosions in the valley, however these will be coming from the quarry up ahead – extracting Westmorland green slate since 1843.

Gaining height, we pass through mixed woodland to the disused *Banks Quarry* and

then onto the open fellside above Langdale. A feature of this walk is the changing view of the Langdale Pikes, really superb from *Brown How*, the rocky knobble that forms the summit of Lingmoor. This is the real reason Heaton Cooper came here – to paint the Pikes; the buzzy bees were a bonus.

The undulating walk over Lingmoor ends at a col with the craggy east face of *Side Pike* directly ahead. We skirt this via a narrow path at the base of the rock, with an improbable squeeze by a detached pillar and gain Side Pike (362m) from the west.

Descending to Great Langdale, where the Hikers' Bar at the Old Dungeon Ghyll Hotel might be a tempting diversion, the return half of the walk is mainly over valley farmland. We pick up the Cumbria Way at *Side House* farm and then follow this for the remaining 5km onto Elterwater. *The return half could be omitted by taking the 'Langdale Rambler' bus from the Old Dungeon Ghyll or by leaving a second car. (Bus enquiries: 0871 200 2233.)*

LINGMOOR FELL & SIDE PIKE

DISTANCE: 12KM/7.5MILES » **TOTAL ASCENT:** 597M/1,959FT » **START GR:** NY 328048 » **TIME:** ALLOW 5 HOURS
MAPS: 2 SHEETS - OS EXPLORER OL7 & OL6, THE ENGLISH LAKES SOUTH-EASTERN AREA & SOUTH-WESTERN AREA, BOTH 1:25,000
REFRESHMENTS: BRITANNIA INN, ELTERWATER: WAINWRIGHTS' INN, CHAPEL STILE: HIKERS' BAR, OLD DUNGEON GHYLL HOTEL
NAVIGATION: TAKE CARE THROUGH THE SLATE WORKINGS AT CHAPEL STILE, WELL SIGNED BUT A WORKING SITE.

CROSSING LINGMOOR

14 LINGMOOR FELL & SIDE PIKE

Directions – Lingmoor Fell & Side Pike

❻ From Elterwater, by Britannia Inn, cross Great Langdale Beck on road bridge. **Turn right** (upstream) on riverside path.

2 After almost 1km, after passing (but NOT crossing) footbridge at rear of Wainwrights' Inn, Chapel Stile, **path swings left**, away from the river, up to quarry workings, passing through a short 'cutting' of stone walls.

3 **Turn right** on reaching tarmac lane and follow footpath signs through site, slate cutting sheds on right. Exit works by site office and into woods. At junction with track (cottage on right), **turn right and immediately left** up path signed *PF Little Langdale*. After about 50m, **turn right** on former quarry track.

4 Track ascends gently, passing disused Banks Quarry. 600m after Banks quarry, **turn sharp left**, on path that zigzags up the fellside; path marked by small cairn and arrow roundel on a short stake. In about 10 minutes reach a locked green iron gate with steps. Climb over and **turn right** up slope to cairn and onward on grassy path between bracken.

5 **Turn right** at T-junction with path coming up from Little Langdale on left. Path ascends with ridge wall on your right to view point with slate bench/windbreak and cairn. Continue around spoil heap and along the undulating fell top.

6 After small tarn near bend in wall, path ascends Brown How, highest point on Lingmoor Fell. Cross stile over wire fence to summit cairn (469m). Path continues NW, at first by fence, but fence soon swings away. Cross knobbly outcrop then steeply down by wallside and over stile. Continue down to col.

7 At col, with Side Pike ahead, cross stile, ascend to foot of the crag and follow path **leftwards** below crag, at one point squeezing between crag and detached pillar. **Take care**, briefly exposed on left. Path ascends rightwards on to Side Pike. On ridge, **fork right** to visit summit (362m), then return to this point and descend worn path westwards, occasional small rocky steps.

> ➤OR *To miss out the 'squeeze' path and Side Pike, **turn left** at **7** and descend directly to road. **Turn right** and follow road to cattle grid at **8**.

8   At road and cattle grid on brow, descend northwards into Great Langdale on engineered path towards woods near campsite (Old Dungeon Ghyll Hotel beyond). Wall and road are to left-hand side while descending. Shortly before reaching wood **turn right** on worn grassy path that dips after passing wood end to join more defined path heading east across fields towards Side House farm.

9   Just above farm, cross ladder stile and footbridge, descend on streamside (do **not** cross to farm) and on eastwards across field. After kissing gate veer up hillside, path cobbled, through old sheepfold, then down. This is the Cumbria Way and waymarked.

10   Junction at Oak Howe, barn and cottage. Follow signed path *PB Gt Langdale Road* past cottage.

11   1km after Oak Howe, cross river at New Bridge on farm track to road*. **Turn right** and follow road through Chapel Stile to just beyond the Wainwrights' Inn. **Turn right**, signed *PF*, and cross footbridge to rejoin outward route at **2**.

> *Do NOT cross New Bridge, instead remain on riverbank path all the way back to Elterwater, rejoining outward route at **2**. This cuts out Chapel Stile but may be awkward immediately downstream from New Bridge where path was partly washed away in 2008.

THE OLD DUNGEON GHYLL HOTEL

CRINKLE CRAGS & PIKE OF BLISCO

DISTANCE: 13KM/8MILES » **TOTAL ASCENT:** 1,100M/3,609FT » **START GR:** NY 286061 » **TIME:** ALLOW 7 HOURS
MAP: OS EXPLORER OL6, THE ENGLISH LAKES SOUTH-WESTERN AREA, 1:25,000 » **REFRESHMENTS:** HIKERS' BAR AT OLD DUNGEON
GHYLL HOTEL » **NAVIGATION:** IN MIST OR CLOUD TAKE CARE AT THREE TARNS AND WHEN LEAVING PIKE OF BLISCO. MAP AND
COMPASS MAY BE NEEDED. PATHS DIVERGE ALONG TOP OF CRINKLE CRAGS, BUT ALL ESSENTIALLY FOLLOW THE RIDGE.

THE BAD STEP, CRINKLE CRAGS

15 Crinkle Crags & Pike of Blisco

13km/8miles

A classic day taking in Hell Gill and the finest ridge top mile in Lakeland.

Old Dungeon Ghyll Hotel » Oxendale » Hell Gill » Three Tarns » Crinkle Crags (859m) » Red Tarn » Pike of Blisco » Redacre Gill » Old Dungeon Ghyll Hotel

Start

National Trust car park by the Old Dungeon Ghyll Hotel at the head of Great Langdale (B5343). GR: NY 286061.

The Walk

The skyline of Crinkle Crags draws the eye of every discerning fellwalker heading up Great Langdale. Above a deeply gashed fellside, broken crags rise to a line of pinnacles that together form one of the finest high-level miles in Lakeland. 'Crinkled' is exactly what it looks, though the name comes from the *Norse Kringla* – a 'circle' – the crags ringing the head of Oxendale.

We start, and perhaps more importantly finish, by the *Old Dungeon Ghyll Hotel*, a favourite watering hole of generations of walkers and climbers. A farm track over fields grazed by indigenous Herdwick sheep leads to *Stool End Farm*. From here we ignore the well-trodden route up The Band and instead turn into *Oxendale* to seek out a quieter way up beside impressive *Whorneyside Force* and the near-subterranean slash of *Hell Gill*.

Soft going up the wide grassy cwm of *Buscoe Sike* brings us back to the Band path and the Great Langdale-Eskdale watershed at *Three Tarns*. Walk over to the nearest tarn and look across the wild expanse of upper Eskdale to the Scafells. Turning south, we embark on the ridge, ascending over stones and rocky 'steps'.

Strictly speaking the first top, with a rock tower, and its higher neighbour, are not 'crinkles' but make up *Shelter Crags* on the OS map. Underfoot it will feel no different. We descend from the second top to a col with a tarn to its SW side and climb the first official crinkle – Gunson Knott.

Hundreds of thousands of boots have worn a multiplicity of lines along the ridge; the terrain is rocky and stony and walkers have strayed as the prevailing wind and fancy for a view (sobering down the gullies on the east face) have taken them. All converge at the cairn on the fourth and highest *Crinkle (Long Top 859m)* and then diverge again – scramblers aiming for 'The Bad Step' and walkers for a westerly diversion.

After the final crinkle we descend easily over the moor to cross the stream flowing out of *Red Tarn* and climb *Pike of Blisco*, weaving up between outcrops to its twin summit. The view down to the Old Dungeon Ghyll Hotel, set below Raven Crag, is almost aerial and our descent there will take another 90 minutes or so, over open fell and then steeply down on made path to *Redacre Gill* and the *Langdale road*.

ON LONG TOP, CRINKLES

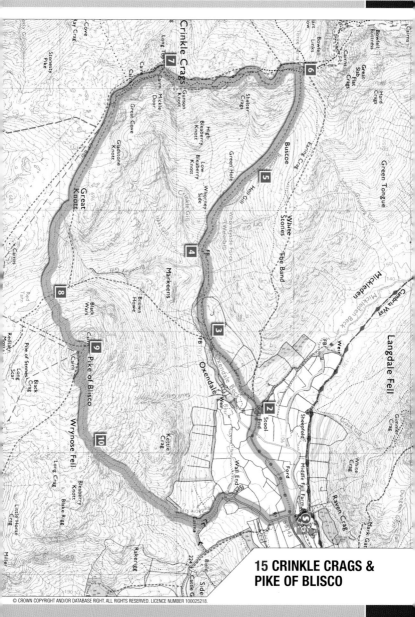

15 CRINKLE CRAGS & PIKE OF BLISCO

Directions – Crinkle Crags &
Pike of Blisco

➎ From the ODGH car park, return to road and **turn right**. When road turns sharp left, **continue ahead** through gate by red post box. Follow tarmac track to Stool End Farm.

2 Through farmyard, path well signed, leaving westwards through gate on broad stony track. At brow continue ahead on lower path (**NOT up right** to The Band).

3 At sheepfold, through gates on to bank of Oxendale Beck. **Do NOT cross footbridge**. Continue with beck on your left, path stony at first, gets rougher with boggy patches.

4 Just after footbridge over side stream flowing from Whorneyside Force (waterfall), **bear right** up grassy ridge; path eroded in places, traversing above waterfalls to ford beck at mouth of Hell Gill. Steeply up on stepped path, Gill to right.

5 At brow (c400m) above Hell Gill, gradient eases. Grassy path up broad cwm of Buscoe Sike, beck away to right, eventually steepening leftwards to meet the main 'Band' path just below Three Tarns col. **Turn left** to col.

6 **Three Tarns** (707m). Broad col between Crinkle Crags and Bow Fell. **Turn southwards** on braided path(s), stony and rocky, on to Shelter Crags and then undulating over the Crinkles.

7 Fourth or Great Crinkle (**Long Top** 859m). Descend either southwards by the scrambly 'Bad Step'* – a 3m wall into a gully (photo page 92) – or strike initially west from the summit cairn and follow path soon swinging leftwards to unite with path descending from Bad Step and continue south to fifth Crinkle. Obvious path continues SE over moor, descending towards Red Tarn.

*Bad Step should only be attempted by competent scramblers.

8 Junction 150m north of Red Tarn. Cross outflow stream and **continue ahead** up flank of Pike of Blisco. Path cairned, zigzagging between outcrops.

9 Pike of Blisco (705m). Twin tops. At notch on summit skyline, **turn left** on to north (highest) top. Return to notch and traverse to south top. Path descends eastwards from just below summit rocks of south top, two short rocky steps warrant **care**.

10 Nearly 1km from top, path crosses stream to cairns on a brow. **Bear left** (NE) and descend on partly stepped path to Redacre Gill and the road (1.3km from cairns). **Turn left**, downhill, to Old Dungeon Ghyll car park.

WHORNEYSIDE FORCE

THE OLD MAN OF CONISTON

DISTANCE: 21KM/13MILES (SEVERAL SHORTCUTS POSSIBLE) **»** **TOTAL ASCENT:** 1,455M/4,774FT **»** **START GR:** SD 304976
TIME: ALLOW 7 TO 8 HOURS FOR FULL ROUND **»** **MAP:** OS EXPLORER OL6, THE ENGLISH LAKES SOUTH-WESTERN AREA,
1:25,000 **»** **REFRESHMENTS:** PUBS AND CAFÉS IN CONISTON **»** **NAVIGATION:** VERY VISIBLE PATHS AND TRACKS ALMOST
THE WHOLE ROUTE. ONLY ON THE ASCENT FROM HOLE RAKE TO WETHERLAM IS THE GRASSY PATH OCCASIONALLY INDISTINCT,
FOLLOWING A BROAD RIDGE.

HEATHERY MINE ENTRANCE, COPPERMINES VALLEY

16 The Old Man of Coniston

High level round of the Coniston Fells.

Coniston village » Miners Bridge » Wetherlam » Swirl Hawse » Swirl How » The Old Man of Coniston (803m) » Goat's Hawse » Dow Crag » Walna Scar Road » Crowberry Haws » Miners Bridge » Coniston village

Start

Car park and Tourist Information Office, off Ruskin Avenue, Coniston village. GR: SD 304976.

The Walk

This is a beefy day, the longest in this book if you do the whole round, with a total ascent well over the height of Ben Nevis. Yet it can be made a good deal shorter while always including the Old Man himself.

Leaving the village, we pass the 16th century *Sun Inn* and head towards *Miners Bridge* and the *Coppermines Valley*. Though Coniston is an archetypal tourist village, the scene that confronts us beyond the bridge is a reminder of an industrial past. For more than 300 years the area's prosperity depended on mining and the price of copper.

Spoil heaps dominate the valley bottom, there is a row of miners' cottages and the manager's home is now a youth hostel. Further up towards Levers Water are many shafts and tunnels. The workings are well worth exploration (keep out of tunnels), but for this round we bear away from the valley, and ascend a broad grassy ridge to the rock cap of *Wetherlam* (762m). Turning west, we lose height to *Swirl Hawse* and ascend the steep ridge of *Prison Band*,

up several rock steps, to the cairn on *Swirl How* (802m). This is the true hub of the Coniston fells. We've come up the east spoke from Wetherlam and now set out on the south spoke – two miles of fine high level walking to the massive slate plinth that crowns *Coniston Old Man*.

A feature of the day is the different panorama at each summit; from Wetherlam the most captivating view is that over Little Langdale; from Swirl How the sterner prospect of the Scafell group; and from the Old Man it is the estuaries of the Kent, Leven and Duddon, and the Irish Sea, surfaced with silver in the afternoon sun.

One more summit awaits, *Dow Crag*, an hour's walk via the col of Goat's Hawse. The highest point is an outcrop of blocks and slabs perched directly above one of the finest climbing crags in Lakeland with the teardrop of Goat's Water at its foot. Continuing south over the subsidiary tops of *Buck Pike* (744m) and *Brown Pike* (682m) we join the *Walna Scar Road*, an ancient track that leads us east over open moorland and eventually to *Coniston*. For the full route there is a loop back to the *Coppermines Valley* to descend via the *Miners Bridge*, but by now the lure of the Sun Inn or simply the journey's end may be too strong.

ON SWIRL HOW

16 THE OLD MAN OF CONISTON

Directions – The Old Man of Coniston

➊ **Turn left** out of car park by Information Office to village centre, cross bridge over Levers Water Beck and **turn right** into lane signed to the Sun Inn. At inn, **turn right**, signed *PF Old Man & Levers Water*. Track passes between buildings, across field and by woods, heading NW.

2 Miners Bridge. Cross bridge over Church Beck and **turn left***. After 100m, just over brow, **bear right** (away from valley bottom) and **right again** at next fork (left fork dips to cottages). Follow track **looping right** towards top of spoil heap and at small cairn **turn left** on small path trending north up fellside.

➋ ***SC**: Cutting out Wetherlam, saving about 150m of ascent and 45 mins. From Miners Bridge continue up main valley bottom track to whitewashed Youth Hostel and on up track to Levers Water. Take path on east side of tarn, ascending grassy hillside to rejoin route at Swirl Hause (**5**).

3 Path enters natural cutting marked on map as Hole Rake. Here **bear left** on a small path that dips across the rake and ascends northwards for 2km to Wetherlam summit. Path indistinct and braided in places, but basically follows broad grassy ridge.

4 **Wetherlam** (762m). From summit cairn descend – steep and stony at first – westwards on cairned path in 1km to col, Swirl Hawse.

5 **Swirl Hawse** (c615m). Col with large pile of stones. Ascend 'Prison Band' ridge path, some rocky steps.

6 **Swirl How** (802m). From summit cairn head south on well-trodden path, dipping to Levers Hawse and on over Brim Fell, to Old Man – 3km in all.

7 **The Old Man of Coniston** (803m). Capped by massive plinth and trig' point. Retrace steps for 100m, then **bear left** (NW) to curve gently downwards above the cwm enclosing Goat's Water.

8 **Goat's Hawse** (649m), col*. Ascend path, initially west then swinging southwards, to the rocky top of Dow Crag (778m). Continue south on ridge over Buck Pike and Brown Pike, then descending SW on made path to join Walna Scar Road (track).

○→ ***SC**: Cutting out Dow Crag. From Goat's Hawse descend path south to Goat's Water and on to Walna Scar Road halfway between points **9** & **10**.

9 At Walna Scar Road, **turn left**, descending eastwards, and follow track for 3km.

10 Track ends at popular parking spot near gate, beyond which a tarmac lane continues for 1.5km down to Coniston village. This is the shortest route to the village. To avoid the tarmac and complete the full circuit, **turn left before the gate** and follow track signed *PF Old Man*.

11 After a little over 1km (about 25 mins walk) track passes through a cutting and bends sharp left, uphill. **We do not**. Instead at bend **turn right**, dropping steeply down and east with the white Youth Hostel in view. Path traverses hillside and descends to the Miners Bridge. Follow outward route back to Coniston village.

SCAFELLS SEEN FROM SWIRL HOW

SECTION 4

West

With Scafell Pike, the highest peak in England, as its pièce de résistance, this is the mountainous heart of the Lake District. There is great variety, from the long, easy ridge from Crag Hill to Causey Pike, to the works of the Emperor Hadrian at Hardknott Castle. Access to the walks in this section is fragmented, with Great Gable and Harter Fell approached from the west coast, Crag Hill from Newlands, and Scafell Pike from the head of Borrowdale.

NAPES NEEDLE, GREAT GABLE (WALK 19)

SESSILE OAK ABOVE RIGG BECK

17 Crag Hill (Eel Crag) & Causey Pike 12.5km/8miles

Steep, little-trodden ascent in wild surroundings to fine skyline hike.

Rigg Beck, Newlands » Addacomb Ridge » Wandope » Crag Hill (839m) » Sail » Causey Pike »
Rowling End » Rigg Beck

Start

Parking at a small, disused quarry on the north side of Rigg Beck bridge, on the Braithwaite-Newlands road.
GR: NY 229202.

The Walk

The compact group of hills that rise between the Newlands Valley and Crummock Water provide fine high level walking. It's more a place of long, clean-limbed ridges, rising steeply over secluded dales than dramatic summits. But one peak does stand out on the approach up the Newlands valley – Causey Pike, diminutive in comparison to the big fellows of this group, yet rearing to command attention. We begin beneath Causey's southern flank and finish over its rocky knobble.

The path up beside *Rigg Beck* is usually quiet and always a pleasure. Up to our right stands one of Lakeland's two rather special high-level woods of sessile oaks. The other is just over the hill to the south, above Keskadale. Both these ancient woods have been studied a good deal by botanists, the oaks forming a low canopy draped across the fell.

Reaching the col, we descend to *Addacomb Beck* and begin the most strenuous part of the day, toiling directly up the hillside to gain the steep ridge that will take us to the top of *Wandope*. While the summit is inconspicuous, the ridge makes an interesting ascent line, affording a bird's eye view into a perfect example of a hanging valley, the wild cwm of Addacomb Hole.

The hard work behind us, we join a well-trodden path up to the trig' point on the summit of *Crag Hill (839m)*, also known as Eel Crag. After a short, scrambly, descent from Crag Hill, the next hour is a treat as we walk the long ridge over *Sail* to *Causey Pike*. The panorama from the pike is good for the full 360 degrees; ridges have been our companions but now the lure is Newlands Valley, pastoral before us. We descend steeply to a path that leads through heather to *Rowling End* and, from this last point on the ridge, sharply down to the Newlands road.

CRAG HILL (EEL CRAG) & CAUSEY PIKE

DISTANCE: 12.5KM/8MILES » **TOTAL ASCENT:** 1,050M/3,445FT » **START GR:** NY 229202 » **TIME:** ALLOW 6 HOURS
MAP: OS EXPLORER OL4, THE ENGLISH LAKES NORTH-WESTERN AREA, 1:25,000 » **REFRESHMENTS:** NONE ALONG ROUTE.
PUBS AT BRAITHWAITE AND SWINSIDE, FARM TEAS AT LITTLE TOWN » **NAVIGATION:** CLEAR PATHS THROUGHOUT EXCEPT FOR
ASCENT FROM ADDACOMB BECK TO WANDOPE WHERE ONE MUST ZIGZAG UP A STEEP GRASSY BANK (BRACKEN IN SUMMER).

ARD CRAGS FROM RIGG BECK PATH

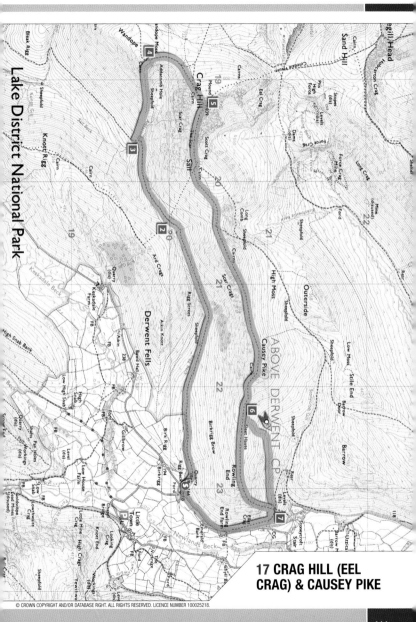

17 CRAG HILL (EEL CRAG) & CAUSEY PIKE

Directions – Crag Hill (Eel Crag) & Causey Pike

➏ From Rigg Beck bridge **take footpath following Rigg Beck upstream** on north bank, *Public Footpath* signpost. Path rises steadily above stream, occasional patches of scree.

2 After 3km path breasts col at c460m and begins descent into valley of Sail Beck. As path curves round hillside, the cwm of Addacomb Hole comes into view with Addacomb Beck falling from its lip. Take a moment to **study the route ahead**: the initially pathless shoulder on the far (southern) side of the beck is the line of ascent.

3 Cross Addacomb Beck, follow the path for another 25m out of the beck hollow and **turn right**, striking uphill on grass and bracken. **No path here**, zigzagging lessens the strain. At about the level of the top of the waterfall / bottom lip of the cwm, a **faint path** appears. Follow this **up the ridge** that forms the southern rim of Addacomb Hole.

4 Addacomb Ridge ends right on the summit of Wandope (772m), marked by a low pile of stones. Follow rim of Addacomb Hole northwards, swinging easterly to join broad path up to the trig' point on Crag Hill.

5 **Crag Hill** (839m). Leave trig' point initially SE to descend the well-named Scar, eroded with short, scrambly bits. Way ahead in full view, broad track stretching eastwards along the ridge top for 2.5km over Sail (773m) and Scar Crag (672m) to Causey Pike. (At Sail Pass a path descends northwards. Ignore this and continue ahead on ridge.)

6 **Causey Pike** (637m). Steepish descent east, scrambly in parts. Continue on heather-fringed ridge path to Rowling End (433m). Descend, path swinging northwards.

➔ ***SC**: At Sleet Hause (460m), below Causey Pike, a path drops left to skirt the northern flank of Rowling End and rejoin the walk at **7**. It does not save any distance but is easier on tired legs than the somewhat awkward descent off Rowling End.

7 At foot of ridge **turn right** on grassy path that curves southwards below Ellas Crag to join the Newlands road above Rowling End Farm. Follow road south for 700m to quarry car park.

HARDKNOTT CASTLE, LOOKING DOWN ESKDALE TO THE IRISH SEA

18 Harter Fell (Eskdale) & Hardknott Castle 8km/5miles

Across a rocky peak to Rome's most lonely outpost – Mediobogdum.

Jubilee Bridge, near Brotherikeld (Eskdale) » Harter Fell (653m) » Hardknott Pass » Hardknott Castle » Jubilee Bridge

Start

Eskdale. Small car park on uphill side of cattle grid at foot of Hardknott Pass, near Brotherikeld. Marked 'Jubilee Bridge' on OS map. GR: NY 213011.

The Walk

Hardknott Castle, in its commanding setting and surviving masonry, is arguably the most impressive Roman fortification in Britain. Arriving at its north-east gate on foot after visiting the delectable Harter Fell, stirs the emotions with a heady mix of romantic history and wild location. The poet Norman Nicholson observed the fort's site on a shelf high above Eskdale was almost impregnable by the military standards of the 2nd century – "but who was going to try and take it anyway?"

We can contemplate such things as we hike up easily from *Jubilee Bridge* on a bridleway that curves around beneath the south flank of *Harter Fell*. Leaving the bridleway to continue its way over to Dunnerdale, we branch uphill on a minor path to the *summit* (653m).

A trig' point at 649m and a cairn mark the fell's westerly top, but the actual summit is the outcrop lying immediately east. This can be climbed in a couple of awkward moves up its cracked west side or more easily by walking round to the east side and ascending a blocky stair. Weather obliging, the view is superb, particularly of the Scafell group to the north and down Eskdale towards the sea. Seemingly at our feet is the square outline of *Hardknott Castle*.

We prospect our way across moorland to the *Hardknott Pass* road, infamous for its 1-in-3 hairpin bends, and walk down a short way before branching off towards the fort, approached in splendid style across a turf plateau that served as a parade ground and in through the north-east gate. Before us are the foundations of the granary, commander's house and other fort buildings. This was *Mediobogdum*, built in the reign of Hadrian and one of the loneliest outposts of his empire. As Nicholson added: "Even the local girls must have been very scarce."

HARTER FELL (ESKDALE) & HARDKNOTT CASTLE

DISTANCE: 8KM/5MILES » **TOTAL ASCENT:** 640M/2,100FT » **START GR:** NY 213011 » **TIME:** ALLOW 3.5 HOURS
MAP: OS EXPLORER OL6 THE ENGLISH LAKES, SOUTH-WESTERN AREA, 1:25,000 » **REFRESHMENTS:** NONE ON ROUTE
NAVIGATION: CLEAR TRACK AND PATH FOR ASCENT. DESCENT LINE FROM SUMMIT TO HARDKNOTT PASS INDISTINCT IN PLACES OVER MOORLAND. MAP AND COMPASS WORK LIKELY TO BE NEEDED IN MIST. IF IN DOUBT, RETURN BY ASCENT PATH.

Directions – Harter Fell & Hardknott Castle

➏ Eskdale. From car park cross beck on footbridge (Jubilee Bridge), signposted *BW to Dunnerdale*, and follow path through a pair of kissing gates and on to good track ascending SW up fellside. After fording stream of Dodknott Gill, go through gate in wall and on to second gate in same wall.

2 Track swings SE after passing through 'second' gate (above). After about 100m **bear left**, leaving track to follow higher path. A small cairn left of the track marks the somewhat indistinct start of this path. At least two more versions of this path leave the track further along. All soon converge as the way steepens; occasional cairns mark the winding ascent.

3 **Harter Fell** (653m). A trig' point at 649m stands on the fell's westerly top. The actual summit is the outcrop lying immediately east. Walk round to its east side and scramble up a blocky stair to the top.

Descent to Hardknott Pass: From the east side of the summit a faint grassy path descends NE over tussocky moor, keeping to the east of Demming Crag. The most used line now follows the left bank of a stream gully (tributary of Castlehow Beck) down to the forest boundary and follows this northward. The OS map indicates a higher line but this is pretty notional on the ground.

4 At the northern end of the forest boundary fence, nearing Hardknott Pass, path crosses stile and soon **swings left** at junction with bridleway and follows this NW to join the Hardknott road on the west side of the pass top. Walk down the road for 300m.

5 At first sharp left-hand bend, **go straight ahead**, signposted *PF*, traversing fellside beneath Border End. After passing second knoll on left, swing downhill to cross broad turf plateau (former Roman parade ground) and enter Hardknott Castle by its NE gateway.

6 Best descent from fort to car park is by path dropping SW. Just before this hits the road, take a squeeze stile through wall and descend to ladder stile at the wall's foot. Cross stile and join road just above car park.

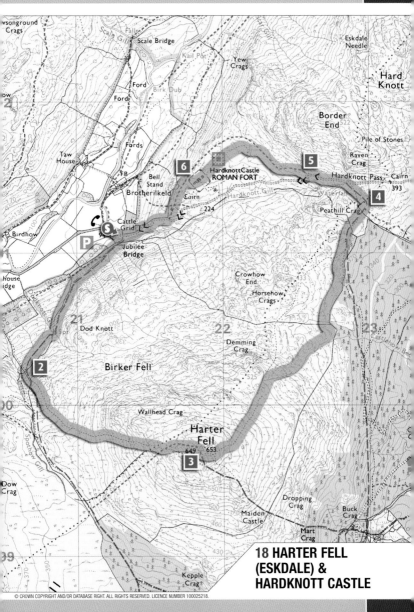

**18 HARTER FELL
(ESKDALE) &
HARDKNOTT CASTLE**

KIRK FELL & GREAT GABLE

DISTANCE: 13KM/8MILES » **TOTAL ASCENT:** 1,153M/3,783FT » **START GR:** NY 187085 » **TIME:** ALLOW 5.5 HOURS
MAPS: OS EXPLORER OL4 THE ENGLISH LAKES, NORTH-WESTERN AREA, AND OL6 SOUTH-WESTERN AREA, BOTH 1:25, 000
REFRESHMENTS: WASDALE HEAD INN » **NAVIGATION:** PATHS FAINT ON SUMMIT AREA OF KIRK FELL. IN POOR VISIBILITY
MAP AND COMPASS WORK MAY BE NECESSARY. ELSEWHERE, PRONOUNCED PATHS AND TRACKS.

WAST WATER AND GREAT GABLE. PHOTO: DAVID CHADWICK

19 Kirk Fell & Great Gable

A grand day out over the lofty guardians of Wasdale.

Wasdale Head » Black Sail Pass » Kirk Fell » Beck Head » Great Gable (899m) » Sty Head » Burnthwaite » Wasdale Head

Start

Parking on Green, 300m before Wasdale Head Inn. GR: NY 187085.

The Walk

The Vikings who settled in Wasdale 1,000 years ago must have found it hauntingly reminiscent of Fjordland. Stand on the shingle shore of Wast Water and the gaze is drawn upwards into a sublime mountain amphitheatre with Yewbarrow, Kirk Fell, Great Gable, Lingmell and the Scafells ringing the head of the dale.

Bands of blue-grey rock buttress Gable's summit and bracken blankets the lower slopes of both Gable and its neighbour, Kirk Fell, our objectives for the day. At their foot, near our starting point, stands the *Wasdale Head Inn*, once home-from-home for the Victorian pioneers of rock climbing and still the mountain inn *par excellence*.

From the rear of the inn, we follow a good track into *Mosedale*, tranquil after the often-busy Green area (starting point for the shortest route up Scafell Pike). Gaining *Black Sail Pass* we turn south and discover that *Kirk Fell* has a craggy side. A ridge and short gully lead to the summit plateau where old iron fence posts are our guide across the stony waste.

We descend from *summit windbreak* (802m) past Kirkfell Tarn and more steeply down Rib End to the col at *Beck Head*. Here we begin a fairly strenuous ascent up the scree and rocks of the north-west ridge. It is not difficult and eventually the angle eases and cairns lead to the summit rocks of *Great Gable* (899m).

Set in the rocks is a bronze plaque depicting in relief the upland, including Gable and Kirk Fell, given by the Fell and Rock Climbing Club to the National Trust as a memorial to Club members killed in the First World War. 20 climbers' names are on the plaque and each year a silent Act of Remembrance is held here. Needless to say, the view is extensive, but best of all is that overlooking Wasdale from Westmorland Cairn, 100m south of the summit. Below, the lattice of stone walls on emerald grass, the farms and whitewashed inn, must be one of the most harmonious creations of humanity working with the grain of nature.

Returning to the summit, we *take care* to select the right line among the rash of cairns and descend on a part-made path to *Sty Head*; from there west on a good path across the south flank of Gable to *Burnthwaite Farm* and finally past the tiny church of St Olaf to *the Green*.

WASDALE FROM FOOT OF NAPES CRAG

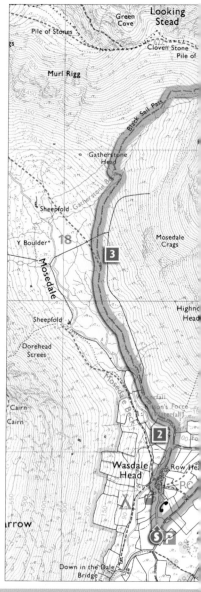

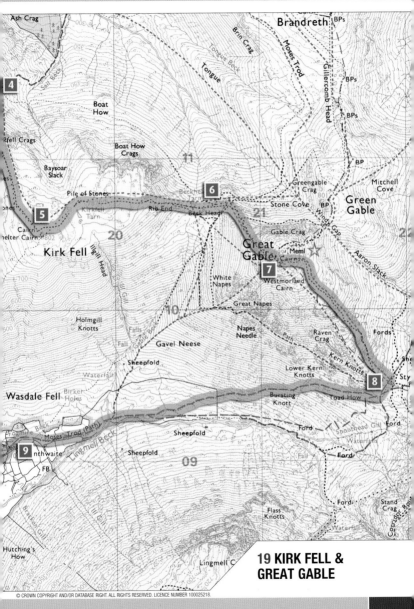

19 KIRK FELL & GREAT GABLE

Directions – Kirk Fell & Great Gable

➌ From the Green, walk up lane to inn, **turn left** in front of Barn Door Shop and **turn right** at Ritson's Bar, north end of inn. Signpost *PB Black Sail Pass*. Take track with beck on left and farm buildings on right. **Do NOT cross beck.**

2 Path ascends bank above stream, through gates, with wall now to left. **Ignore track branching right** and also path up fell nose. Through gate on brow and on up Mosedale.

3 At cairn (pile of stones) **bear right on main path** rising towards distant gate. (Lesser path continues in valley bottom.) Through gate, onward to ford Gatherstone Beck and ascend on partly engineered path towards pass.

4 **Black Sail Pass** (542m). At cairn on pass, **turn right** (briefly SE) across grass and up worn path towards foot of rocky spur. Ascend stony/scree path on left (facing) side of spur. At foot of bouldery gully path bears left beneath broken crags and ascends via a shorter, easy gully to fell plateau.

5 **Kirk Fell**. On gaining plateau head SSE for 700m to summit cairns and windbreak (802m). In poor visibility, a line of old iron fence posts, starting just to right of gully top, is a sure guide to the summit. From windbreak, go ENE to Kirkfell Tarn and by a small subsidiary top (787m), then **east** to Rib End where not very obvious cairns mark a rough descent path to Beckhead Tarn.

6 **Beck Head** (620m). From tarn continue east on col to staggered junction of bigger paths coming up on right from Wasdale and leftwards over skyline from Stone Cove. Ascend SE on well cairned line up stony and bouldery end of Great Gable. Hard work.

7 **Great Gable** (899m). From the summit rocks descend SE on cairned path to Sty Head. **Take care** on leaving summit to get the right line. Several routes converge up here and there is a rash of cairns. The path is well trodden and engineered for much of its 1.2km.

8 Sty Head. At the mountain rescue Stretcher Box, **turn sharp right** to cairn and path that turns the foot of the ridge of Gable and then descends westwards at a comfortable angle – 2.5km from Sty Head to Burnthwaite farm.

9 Burnthwaite. At rear of farm, go through gate on your left into yard, then right by end of farm and follow lane for almost 1km to the Green, passing St Olaf's Church.

FELL AND ROCK CLIMBING CLUB MEMORIAL

SCAFELL PIKE

DISTANCE: 15KM/9.5MILES » **TOTAL ASCENT:** 1,069M/3,507FT » **START GR:** NY 236122 » **TIME:** ALLOW 6.5 HOURS
MAPS: 2 SHEETS – OS EXPLORER OL4 & OL6, THE ENGLISH LAKES NORTH-WESTERN AREA & SOUTH-WESTERN AREA, BOTH
1:25,000 » **REFRESHMENTS:** SEASONAL TEAROOM AT SEATHWAITE FARM; NEAREST BAR AT SCAFELL HOTEL, ROSTHWAITE
NAVIGATION: SUMMIT AREA OF BROAD CRAG AND SCAFELL PIKE IS A BOULDER FIELD, 'PATH' NOT ALWAYS CLEAR BUT ROUTE
LINE IS CAIRNED. CAREFUL ATTENTION NEEDED IN POOR VISIBILITY, ABILITY TO USE A MAP AND COMPASS ESSENTIAL

ON SCAFELL PIKE, WAST WATER AND IRISH SEA BEYOND

20 Scafell Pike

Across the highest peak in England – a full-on mountain day.

Seathwaite (Borrowdale) » Stockley Bridge » Grains Gill » Esk Hause » Broad Crag » Scafell Pike (978m) » Corridor Route » Sty Head » Stockley Bridge » Seathwaite

Start

Seathwaite at the head of Borrowdale, parking on lane-side approaching farm. GR: NY 236122.

The Walk

Scafell Pike is a challenging proposition and definitely a full day's outing. You'd expect nothing less of the highest mountain in England. If at all possible save it for a clear day – why go to all that effort to see only cloud or rain? And certainly give it a miss in bad weather. The whole of the massif from Broad Crag to the summit cairn is covered in boulders and stones, awkward under foot in the best of conditions and tricky to navigate over in bad visibility. On all sides are crags or steep, rough ground.

Of course, those factors that lend a degree of seriousness to the ascent of Scafell Pike are the same ones that make it such a satisfying mountain day. This is rugged country and this round from Seathwaite at the head of Borrowdale makes the very best of it.

The day begins benignly enough, through the farm at *Seathwaite* and up the valley track to *Stockley Bridge*, a classic packhorse bridge arching over the beck of Grains Gill. Continuing south up *Grains*, the path steepens and soon after passing the ravine

of Ruddy Gill we reach the walkers' highway between Wasdale and Great Langdale. Directly ahead are the buttresses and gullies of Great End, a playground for winter climbers when draped in snow and ice.

Skirting Great End we reach *Esk Hause* and get our first sight of the wilds of upper Eskdale. As we curve up *Calf Cove* and pick a way across the boulder field between *Broad Crag* and *Ill Crag*, the cairn-cum-platform on the top of *Scafell Pike* comes into view, but at still some distance. We lose height, dropping steeply to a col before zigzagging up to the summit (978m). *Take care* on the skittery stones up from the col.

Needless to say, the view is extensive. We can sit for a while gazing out across West Water to a coastline besmirched by the chimneys of the Sellafield nuclear plant, and beyond that the hazy outline of the Isle of Man.

We descend via *Lingmell* col to the *Corridor Route*, a path of character that winds along the rough western flank of Broad Crag and Great End, and eventually to *Sty Head*. From here we turn down by *Sty Head Tarn* and on to *Stockley Bridge*, rejoining our outward route, weary but with a deserved sense of achievement.

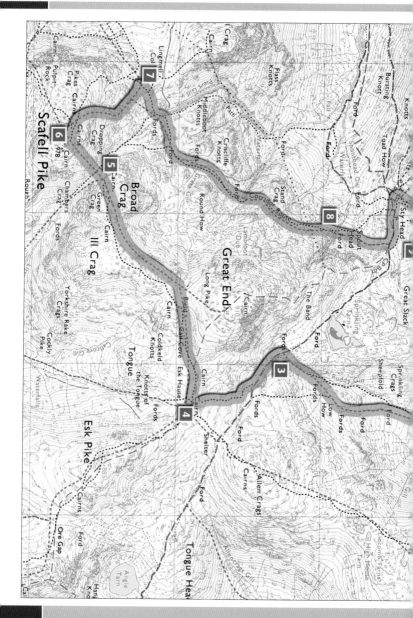

20 SCAFELL PIKE

Directions – Scafell Pike

⊙→ At Seathwaite, walk through farm, whitewashed farmhouse and cottages on left, and continue south on valley track signed *PF Esk Hause and PB Styhead*.

2 Stockley Bridge. Cross stone bridge, go through gate and **immediately turn left** alongside wall. Continue up Grains Gill valley for 2km on good path, steepening above chasm of Ruddy Gill.

3 Cairn as path crests the top of the gill; ford beck to junction with main Wasdale-Great Langdale path. **Turn left** and in 400 metres (about 10 minutes) **at fork bear right**. Path angles uphill.

4 Esk Hause (col between Great End and Esk Pike). Large pile of stones and view south over Upper Eskdale. **Turn right** (west) on cairned path to Calf Cove and up to col on south side of Great End. Path trends leftwards, ascending bouldery slopes of Broad Crag – awkward underfoot, watch for small cairns.

5 Steep rocky descent to col between Broad Crag and Scafell Pike. Loose stony path ascends in zigzags to Pike.

> ⚠ **Warning**: In snow or ice this ascent can be hazardous and ice axe and crampons are advisable.

6 **Scafell Pike** (978m). Ascend stony slope to big summit plinth and survey cairn. Leave summit by cairned line NW on survey cairn side of plinth. Aim for large cairn on brow.

7 **Key junction**. Path divides at cairn at c755m, overlooking Lingmell col. Ground is stony and path indistinct. **Fork right**, aim for Sty Head Tarn in distance. (Leftwards goes to Hollow Stones.) Path traverses stony ground to cairn on brow then descends to cross the stream above Piers Gill. **Take care** here traversing the shelving rock high above gill. Exposed section lasts only a few metres to a fork in the path. **Bear right** around hillside, winding northwards on the Corridor Route.

8 Skew Gill. Just after crossing stream, take care as path traverses above Gill to arrive at the foot of rock step. Ascent line marked with an arrow scratched on the rock. Path resumes above, generally descending until a rise to **9**.

9 Junction with main Wasdale-Great Langdale path. **Turn left**, descending to **Sty Head**. At Stretcher Box **turn right** on broad path passing to west side of Sty Head Tarn. **Cross footbridge** and continue on streamside, stony at first. Path soon becomes well defined again and descends steadily to Stockley Bridge (2.5km from Sty Head to Stockley Bridge). Follow outward track back to Seathwaite.

ICED CAIRN, SCAFELL PIKE, LOOKING NW

Appendix

The following is a list of Tourist Information Centres, shops, cafes, pubs, websites and other contacts that might come in handy.

Tourist Information Centres

www.lake-district.gov.uk – Official website of the Lake District National Park.

Ambleside	T: 01539 432 582
Carlisle	T: 01228 512 444
Coniston	T: 01539 441 533
Grasmere	T: 01539 435 245
Kendal	T: 01539 725 758
Keswick	T: 01768 772 645
Penrith	T: 01768 867 466
Seatoller, Borrowdale	T: 01768 777 294
Ullswater	T: 01768 482 414
Windermere	T: 01539 446 499

Food and Drink
Cafes

(See individual routes for recommendations.)

Shepherd's 'Caff', High Lodore Farm, Borrowdale
T: 01768 777 221

Wilf's, Staveley	T: 01539 822 329
Bluebird Café, Coniston	T: 01539 441 649

The Old Sawmill Tearoom, Mirehouse
T: 01768 774 317

Fellbites, Glenridding	T: 01768 482 781
Rydal Hall Tea Room, Rydal	T: 01539 432 050

Pubs

(See individual routes for recommendations.)

Golden Rule, Ambleside	T: 01539 433 363

Old Dungeon Ghyll Hotel, Gt Langdale
T: 01539 437 272

The Mill Inn, Mungrisdale	T: 01768 779 632
Travellers Rest, Glenridding	T: 01768 482 298
Brotherswater Inn, Patterdale	T: 01768 482 239
The Wasdale Head Inn	T: 01946 726 229
Wainwrights' Inn, Chapel Stile	T: 01539 438 088

Accommodation
Youth Hostels

YHA Youth Hostels can be found in the following places. For more information please visit www.yha.org.uk

Ambleside	T: 0845 371 9620
Borrowdale	T: 0845 371 9624
Coniston (Coppermines)	T: 0845 371 9630
Derwent Water	T: 0845 371 9314
Grasmere (Butharlyp Howe)	T: 0845 371 9319
Helvellyn	T: 0845 371 9742
Kendal	T: 0845 371 9641
Keswick	T: 0845 371 9746
Langdale	T: 0845 371 9748
Skiddaw House	T: 07747 174 293
Wasdale	T: 0845 371 9350
Windermere	T: 0845 371 9352

Bunkhouses, B&Bs and Hotels

www.staylakedistrict.co.uk

For specific information, contact a Tourist Information Centre in the area in which you intend to stay.

Camping

Wasdale Head Campsite   T: 01946 726 220
There are many more campsites in the Lake
District – simply call a Tourist Information Centre
in the area where you intend to stay.

Weather

www.metoffice.gov.uk   www.mwis.org.uk

Outdoor Shops

Needle Sports
www.needlesports.com   T: 01768 772 227
Keswick

George Fisher Ltd
www.georgefisheronline.co.uk T: 01768 772 178
Keswick

Cotswold Outdoor
www.cotswoldoutdoor.com T: 01768 781 030
Keswick

The Climbers Shop
www.climbers-shop.com   T: 01539 432 297
Ambleside

Stewart Cunningham
www.srcunningham.co.uk   T: 01539 432 636
Ambleside

The Barn Door Shop
www.barndoorshop.co.uk   T: 01946 726 384
Wasdale Head

Penrith Outdoor Pursuits
www.penrithoutdoorpursuits.com
T: 01768 891 383
Penrith

Freetime
www.freetime1.co.uk   T: 01228 598 210
Carlisle

Nevisport
www.nevisport.com   T: 01539 734 428
Kendal

Other Contacts

Cumbria Tourism   www.golakes.co.uk

Other Publications

Day Walks in the Peak District
Norman Taylor and Barry Pope, Vertebrate
Publishing – **www.v-publishing.co.uk**

Day Walks in the Yorkshire Dales
Bernard Newman, Vertebrate Publishing –
www.v-publishing.co.uk

Lake District Mountain Biking – Essential Trails
Chris Gore and Richard Staton, Vertebrate
Publishing – **www.v-publishing.co.uk**

Mountain Biking Trail Centres – The Guide
Tom Fenton, Vertebrate Publishing –
www.v-publishing.co.uk

About the Author

Stephen Goodwin is a freelance journalist and editor of the prestigious *Alpine Journal*. He turned freelance in 1999 after 13 years as a staffer on *The Independent*, mainly covering politics at Westminster. A climber and ski-mountaineer, in 1998 he reached the south summit of Everest, filing an award-winning diary to *The Independent*. Since then, he has returned to the Himalaya most years as well as forays into the Alps, Andes and Turkey. Yet for all this exotica, he finds equal pleasure in walking and climbing in the Lake District, a stone's throw from his home in Cumbria's lovely Eden Valley.

Vertebrate Publishing

Vertebrate Publishing an independent publisher dedicated to producing the very best outdoor leisure titles. We have critically acclaimed and award-winning titles covering a range of leisure activities, including; mountain biking, cycling, rock climbing, hill walking and others. We are best known forour own titles such as *Lake District Mountain Biking*, and *Revelations* – the autobiography of British rock climber Jerry Moffatt, awarded the **Grand Prize** at the **2009 Banff Mountain Book Festival**.

For more information about Vertebrate Publishing please visit our website: **www.v-publishing.co.uk**

Perfect for the Lakes

www.rab.uk.com